My Best Men are Women

Also by Flora Larsson

FLORA LARSSON

My Best Men are Women

HODDER AND STOUGHTON
LONDON SYDNEY AUCKLAND TORONTO

TO THE
VALIANT WOMEN OFFICERS
UNNAMED
IN THIS BOOK

Contents

Personalia

Preface

WHILE writing this book I have been haunted by women. An invading multitude of my own sex has thronged my home, accompanying me in all my waking hours. I have been inspired by women, plagued by women, thrilled by women, nearly drowned in a sea of women.

In my ardour to do at least a modicum of justice to the heroic band of Salvation Army women, I gathered a bouquet of over a hundred names, but later felt that so many in one feast would create a kind of woman-indigestion. Some must be deleted,

I clenched my teeth, brandished my kitchen scissors and cut out one half of them! I felt like a murderess. The headless ones that I had guillotined lay around me, their paper corpses mute witness to my hard-heartedness. Even today they lie heavy on my heart, the unnamed ones.

At night the cohorts of women invaded my dreams. Among others I saw a Chinese woman. Pale, drawn of face, and seemingly under stress, she glided into my field of vision. I saw the Army emblems on her grey uniform, which looked worn and threadbare. Her thin face neared mine and I whispered, 'I'd like to tell your story but I don't know your name.' She drifted past me and vanished, murmuring, 'My name is known to God.'

All my women wear bonnets, large bonnets like coal-scuttles

or tiny bonnets half hidden by a modern hair style. Vivacious women, quiet women; some educated, others rough and ready; some heartily healthy, others delicate; but all sharing a common dedication to God's service under the Army flag. The Divine Fisherman flung out His bait and in their youthful zeal they snapped at it. Swiftly the divine reel was wound in, for the hook had entered into their souls. They were caught ... for life. Evangelists, slum-sisters, writers, home-mothers, nurses, teachers, administrators, they march in closed ranks with heads held high, worthy of the great traditions of the past. Theirs has been no dainty discipleship but rather a stern involvement costing 'blood, sweat and tears'.

Central among them is Catherine Booth, the Army Mother, her sweetly-serious face framed in her small bonnet. She opened the door into female ministry for her daughter-salvationists of the coming generations. She gave them the right to preach, to break the Bread of Life to hungry souls, to be servants of all for Christ's sake. From the ramparts of heaven she watches over them with tender yet proud mother-heart.

I send out these vignettes of women officers of The Salvation Army to meet the friendly or critical eyes of readers who may assess them as they wish, but judged by the values of the Kingdom of Heaven they shine as true gold. For any errors in the telling of their stories the author must bear responsibility.

FLORA LARSSON

CHAPTER ONE

A Woman in the Pulpit

'I WANT to say a word . . .'

A woman is speaking. A woman wants to be heard in public. Her request should strike an echoing note in the minds of women today, although the event took place more than a hundred years ago. This woman is Catherine Booth, later to be known as the Mother of The Salvation Army.

To state that the incident occurred because of bad weather on that particular Sunday would only be surmise. It would have happened somewhere, sometime, for a volcanic fire was burning in Catherine's heart, throbbing, pulsing, rising towards the moment when the depths of her being would release the pent-up forces within.

The scene was the Bethesda Chapel, Gateshead, on Whit Sunday, 1860. The crowd of more than a thousand who had gathered there felt a certain sense of disappointment. The day was to have been celebrated by a giant service in the open at Windmill Hill, but the gusty, inclement weather had driven the shivering people into the chapel. Catherine sat in the minister's pew as was her right, her four-year-old son by her side. Five years before, at the age of twenty-six, she had been married to the fiery evangelist William Booth and with him had shared many varied scenes and temporary homes.

Later on, telling of the incident, Catherine said,

It seemed as if a voice said to me, 'Now if you were to go and testify, you know I would bless it to your own soul as well as to the souls of the people.' I gasped and said in my soul . . . 'I cannot do it.' And then the devil said, 'Besides, you are not prepared to speak. You will look like a fool and have nothing to say.' He made a mistake! He overdid himself for once! It was that word that settled it. I said, 'Ah! this is just the point. I have never yet been willing to be a fool for Christ. *Now I will be one!'*

Just as William Booth concluded his sermon Catherine, pale but determined, rose from her place and advanced towards the pulpit. William was startled at this intrusion into the service but also puzzled, knowing his wife's timid nature in public.

Stepping down from the pulpit he enquired, 'What is the the matter, my dear?'

'I want to say a word . . .' The living volcano in Catherine's heart had burst its way out to liberty, with results such as even she at that moment could not foretell.

'My wife wants to say a word.' Dazed by the turn of events, William gallantly stood aside to let his wife mount the pulpit steps for the first time, but certainly not for the last. What were Catherine's feelings as she faced that large audience?

I got up there — God only knows how — and if any mortal ever did hang on the arm of Omnipotence, I did. I just told the people how it came about. I said, 'I daresay many of you have been looking upon me as a very devoted woman . . . but I have been living in disobedience.'

She went on to tell how God's Spirit had been urging her to preach the gospel publicly and how she had promised Him she would do so a few months ago when her second little daughter was born. Yet time had passed and she had been silent. She dared no longer disobey.

By the time Mrs. Booth had finished speaking the people were visibly moved, many weeping audibly as she made her way back to her place. William, her husband, showed that mastery of a situation which was one of his dominant characteristics throughout life. With reckless liberality he announced, 'My wife will preach this evening.' Catherine was launched on her public career and from that clever mind and burning heart such streams of dedicated oratory were to burst forth as would make her world-renowned.

Already for a number of years Catherine Booth had been woman's staunch ally, using her analytical mind and astounding command of language on behalf of her sex. Even into her love-letters to William she wove the tapestry of the absorbing theme of how women can be used to their fullest potential.

God has given to women a graceful form and attitude, winning manners, persuasive speech, and above all, a finely toned emotional nature, all of which appear to us eminent qualifications for public speaking ... I believe that one of the greatest boons to the race would be woman's exaltation to her proper position, mentally and spiritually. Who can tell its consequences to posterity? If indeed there is in Jesus Christ 'neither male nor female' but in all touching His Kingdom they are one, who shall dare thrust woman out of the church's operations or presume to put any candle which God has lighted under a bushel? Why should the swaddling bands of blind custom ... be again wrapped round the female disciples of the Lord?

After many pages of the same passionate pleading for the use of women in the proclaiming of the gospel, Catherine added the surprising statement, 'You *know* nothing I have said is to be interpreted personally.' There was the rub. That had been Catherine's secret defeat. She was ready to espouse woman's cause but not yet to be offered on the altar of that cause.

Not only in her extensive love-letters did Catherine Booth press for women's right to preach the gospel. She addressed a sharp two-thousand-word letter to her own minister who had made some derogatory remarks about woman as a moral being. A year later she published an article on the same flaming theme and followed it up with the eleven-thousand-word pamphlet on 'Female Ministry' which will ever be associated with her name.

How strange that this dedicated apostle should be firing all her heavy guns from the rear instead of leading the troops into battle! The day was soon to dawn when she would exchange the pen for the pulpit. God had been long preparing His chosen vessel and His urgings and pressures brought out the quietly uttered yet tremendously important phrase, 'I want to say a word.'

In the very year that she spoke those words, 1860, Catherine had prophesied, 'Whether the church will allow women to speak in her assemblies can only be a matter of time.' Catherine's time had come!

She was thirty-one, half-way through her life-span. She had been a writer, a most prolific writer, a mode of expression more suited to her retiring nature than the public platform. For the second half of her life the spoken word would take precedence over the written. She had become a preacher of the gospel. What it would demand of her, physically and spiritually, she could not envisage. It was not only that she was endowed with a logical, well-equipped mind and an acceptable, persuasive delivery. On those two counts alone her gifts must be regarded as truly remarkable. But hers was a passionate, loving heart. There cascaded from the deeps of her being such a stream of outgoing love that all felt the force of it. Barriers of sin and indifference were swept away by the torrent of her fervent involvement in the saving of souls. It was costly giving.

Later Catherine was to confess, 'I was never allowed to have another quiet Sabbath when I was well enough to stand and speak.'

On that Whit Sunday in Gateshead in 1860 Catherine Booth opened a door for the women of the yet unborn Salvation Army, a door through which they would march with heads held high, preachers of the Word of God to needy souls the world over.

The first woman evangelist was given responsibility for a centre in 1875. This was referred to as a daring experiment. A further comment stated that:

It has sometimes been said that female preachers would be the ruin of the Mission. But on the contrary, it turns out that the prosperity of the work in every respect just appears most precisely at the very time when female preachers are being allowed the fullest opportunity.

The door of pastoral ministry that Catherine Booth had opened was now thrown wide to the women of The Salvation Army. A list of its evangelical stations published in 1878 showed that of ninety-one officers on the field, forty-one were women.

William Booth, though at first only lukewarm in response to his wife's valiant championing of her sex, was soon won over by the successes of the women. Once having taken that position, he resolutely upheld and enforced it. The expanding Army needed a manual of guidance to ensure that its progress continued along intended lines. He set about preparing a considerable tome of Regulations for Salvation Army Officers which is still in use in amended form. It contains a chapter on the position of women. It is a short chapter, only one and a half pages. Here are its salient points:

Women have the right to an equal share with men in the work of publishing salvation.

A woman may hold any position of authority or power in the Army.

A woman is not to be kept back from any position of power or influence merely on account of her sex.

Women must be treated as equal with men in all the intellectual and social relationships in life.

With this charter Army women were launched into warfare against evil and service for mankind by the side of their male colleagues. The following chapters give glimpses of how they have acquitted themselves.

They have not followed an identical pattern. Through special qualifications or a sense of calling, sometimes by direct orders from their leaders, they have developed along diverging avenues of usefulness, fanning out from the central unifying point of the total commitment of their lives to God's service in The Salvation Army. Their aim is the same in all branches of work. It is to win people for God by direct exhortation or by loving, caring ministry. In the hour of consecration to their life-task they have made Albert Orsborn's words their own:

My life must be Christ's broken bread,
My love His outpoured wine,
A cup o'erfilled, a table spread
Beneath His name and sign,
That other souls, refreshed and fed,
May share His life through mine.

CHAPTER TWO

God's Teenage Militants

TEENAGERS of today may feel that they have achieved a new status where they can express their views and expect to be heard. They might be very surprised to know what teenagers accomplished a hundred years ago.

In the Army's early days young girls took on responsibilities that might well have daunted an older woman. A seventeen-year-old girl was sent in charge of a new Army opening in Pentre, Wales, and the result was a powerful religious revival among the miners and their families in the Rhondda Valley. Hundreds of men were converted, and one report added the enlightening fact that 'in one colliery the very horses can't make out what has happened, the treatment they now receive is so different.'

On Tyneside a similar remarkable phenomenon occurred through the ministry of girl salvationists. From Gateshead it was reported that so many men had been converted that the police charge-sheet was reduced by fifty per cent.

W. T. Stead, London journalist and good friend of William and Catherine Booth, learned of the exploits of 'two Hallelujah lassies' at Darlington through his farm-hand. The reports were so startling that Stead felt he must investigate for himself.

I was amazed [he wrote]. I found two delicate girls, one

hardly able to write a letter, the other not yet nineteen, ministering to a crowded congregation which they had themselves collected out of the street, and building up an aggressive church militant out of the human refuse which other churches regarded with blank despair. In the first six months a thousand persons had been down to the Penitent Form; many of them had joined various religious organisations in the town, and a corps or a church was formed of nearly two hundred members, each of whom was pledged to speak, pray, sing, visit, march in procession and take a collection, or do anything that wanted doing.

Teenage conversions are a well-known phenomenon and young Eliza Shirley fitted into that pattern. No one could have foreseen what heroic service the girl kneeling at the Army Penitent Form would render. Her parents, too, had been converted and all three were soldiers of the Coventry corps. Eliza was on fire for God and offered herself to William Booth for full-time service, being accepted as an officer in 1879 and given the rank of lieutenant although only sixteen years of age.

The family economy was wavering, so father Shirley decided to emigrate to America with his wife and daughter. The only difficulty was that Eliza, as an officer, was under orders to stay in her appointment. She wrote to the General (William Booth from being general superintendent of the Christian Mission had by a simple transition become general of the newly-named Salvation Army), asking for leave to accompany her parents to America. The General was not pleased at the prospect of losing so good and promising a young officer, but added in his letter,

If you must go and if you should start a work, start it on the principles of The Salvation Army, and if it is a success we may see our way to take it over.

Cautious General Booth! With hindsight we can charge him with lack of vision of what was to come — his own daughter Evangeline at the head of thousands of American salvationists — but Booth at that time had many problems with his rapidly expanding Army.

In Philadelphia, where the Shirleys decided to make their home, Eliza and her mother tried to find a hall where they could hold meetings on Army lines. The only possibility seemed to be a dilapidated old building, formerly a furniture factory. Hearing for what purpose they wished to rent the property, the agent gave them a curt refusal.

Eliza's photograph at sixteen reveals a broad face with plenty of character in its contours. That inward steel plus her faith in God made her say, 'Think it over. We'll be back tomorrow.'

The Shirley family, all three of them, concentrated on praying. True, the building they had seen was in a shocking condition, but it was the only one available. When Eliza and her mother called on the agent next morning he had changed his mind and would rent it to them for ten dollars a month. '*God* changed his mind,' commented Eliza happily as they trudged home.

Preparing the property as a meeting-hall was an adventure on its own. Gaping holes in the roof had to be covered over, broken windows replaced. The floor was only trampled dirt, but it could be covered with clean sawdust. Grimy walls benefited by a coat of whitewash. A friend lent father Shirley money to buy a few benches and sufficient planks of wood to cover part of the floor, at least where speakers would stand and penitents would kneel. The 'salvation factory', as they called it, was ready for opening. Glaring posters soon made it known to the residents.

> Blood and Fire! The Salvation Army
> Two Hallelujah females
> will speak and sing for Jesus
> in the old chair factory
> at Sixth and Oxford Streets
> Oct. 5th at 11 a.m. 3 p.m. 8 p.m.
> All are invited to attend.

Such flamboyant advertising should have produced a crowd, but the three Shirleys found only twelve people waiting to hear of the redemptive love of God. The start was cool, but it soon warmed up when a notorious drunkard was converted. Visiting Philadelphia a few weeks later, a reporter described the scene:

> Two women, both good-looking, who were dressed in black, conducting their meeting, assisted by the male and other female members of the band. The two 'Hallelujah females' heading the line, with faces towards it and walking backward, led the procession down German Town Road singing a rousing hymn. Crowds collected on every corner, and windows and doorways were filled with spectators while it moved along followed by almost everything that had legs. Every bench in the factory was filled . . . every foot of standing room was taken.

A plaque marks the spot where Lieutenant Eliza won her first victories on American soil and it is interesting to learn that five of her direct descendants are Army officers. There was good stuff in the sixteen-year-old pioneer.

When the work was well established in the old chair factory, Eliza's parents took charge with the rank of captain, while she opened another evangelical centre in West Philadelphia. Widowed soon afterwards, Eliza's mother pioneered Salvation Army operations in Canada and later became the first woman divisional officer in the United States. A remarkable mother and daughter.

Eighteen months later Commissioner Railton, one of William Booth's most trusted helpers, was sent to New York with a team of *seven women* and a £200 cheque to start Army work there. Railton himself chose women as his co-workers, and named them the Splendid Seven. At the departure of the team one original officer, Captain Cadman, seized the unique occasion for a special 'farewell of the Yankees'. He concluded the meeting by praying, 'Lord, these ladies are going to America to preach the gospel. If they are fully given up to Thee, be with them and bless them and grant them success. But if they are not faithful, drown 'em, Lord, drown 'em!'

The Lord did not drown them but He came very near to doing so, for one of the ship's cylinders broke and stormy weather kept the seasick soldiers on their backs for most of the twenty-six days' voyage. A stone tablet at Battery Point Pier commemorates the first open-air meeting of the Splendid Seven and their leader, held immediately after disembarkation. Their number had increased by one lad convert gained during the voyage. He held the flag which had been presented to them by Mrs. Booth and which bore the visionary wording 'New York nr. 1.'

*   *   *

Another teenage girl who had a remarkable whirlwind career was Augusta Lindblad of Sweden. Converted at fourteen in an

Army meeting, she served in the local corps before seeking officership in July 1886. Augusta's mother had studied the Army doctrines and found them acceptable, but she did not like the red jerseys which salvationists wore then as uniform. She consulted a Lutheran priest known for evangelical sympathies. 'Isn't it pharisaical to dress up like that?' she asked him. 'No,' replied the priest, 'they witness for God in their red jerseys.' So Augusta was allowed to wear one, with a bonnet topping her dark hair. At fifteen she was a cadet in training. At sixteen she was promoted captain and sent to the large corps in Linköping which was housed in a theatre.

Augusta was a born leader. She gave orders and expected to be obeyed. Two long plaits hung down her back emphasising her youth, but she maintained dynamic leadership over a hundred salvation soldiers. Night after night she preached to great crowds.

Full of initiative, she decided to profit by the great influx of farmers on market-day to arrange a midday meeting which they could attend when business was finished. Wearing large posters over her shoulders and followed by two other women equally well decorated, she stalked around the market square, weaving her way in and out of the gaping crowds. Her ruse succeeded. Many farmers came to the noon meeting to hear her preach and to receive a challenge from God which they could ponder as they jogged homewards.

One day a man approached Augusta and introduced himself as the mayor. He asked her to try to help a man who had been in prison many times for wife-beating. He was soon to be discharged and his poor wife shivered with apprehension as she waited. The Captain promised to do her best. She found the woman crouching in the corner of a dark room, dulled with fright. In tense whispers she explained why her husband was serving the present sentence. Their backyard adjoined that of the police inspector. One day as the man was beating his wife, the inspector heard the blows and cries and called over the fence for him to stop. That made him even more irate. 'If you want her, you can have her,' he sneered, and threw the poor woman over the fence into the neighbouring yard.

Having learnt when the husband was expected home from prison, Augusta arrived in good time, accompanied by her lieutenant, both with guitars. The man was startled to find such a reception committee awaiting him and he seemed to soften as the two girls sang and spoke. Before leaving they prayed with him.

That night he came to the meeting. When the sermon ended with an invitation for immediate decision, he went forward to the Penitent Form where one of God's miracles took place. He not only experienced forgiveness of sin but was also transformed, as his life witnessed afterwards. A few months later Augusta had the joy of enrolling both him and his wife as salvation soldiers. To express his great appreciation the mayor donated fifty crowns to the self-denial fund!

Later that year Augusta Lindblad received her farewell orders, as they are termed: instructions to move to a new appointment. The local station-master granted her permission to hold a final meeting by the train before departure. Crowds packed the station. Bandsmen, soldiers, converts and friends all waved and cheered as the seventeen-year-old captain clambered on to a wooden box to give her last charge to them and to commend her spiritual children to the Lord.

Her new task was to open a corps at Jönköping where the Army had hired a riding-school building with seating for two thousand. It was filled night after night, so packed that the two girl officers had to elbow their way on to the platform to speak.

It still smelt strongly of horses! In five months hundreds had been converted, many of them former drunkards. Eighteen youths from the grammar school had also been saved. The young captain understood that she could not visit them in their homes or lodgings, so she asked the local Lutheran priest to give them spiritual help, which he did very willingly. Some of these lads became priests in the State Church and others became Army officers.

Once more farewell orders reached Captain Augusta Lindblad, this time taking her to Kristiania, Norway's capital, now Oslo. From Sweden the Army had moved over the frontier to pioneer in Norway.

The same spiritual success crowned Augusta's service in the new sphere for twelve months; then she was transferred back to Stockholm, soon afterwards to join heart and career in marriage with Staff-Captain Andersson.

      *   *   *

In England the young Salvation Army was developing with amazing rapidity. Calls were already coming from other lands. The first handful of Army officers were working in the United States and Australia. Now came letters from all parts of France entreating the Army to come, asking when the Army would come, or warning the Army not to come. From one group came the strange assurance that they were praying God to keep The Salvation Army out of France.

That prayer was not granted!

It had finally been decided. Katie, eldest daughter of William and Catherine Booth, only twenty-two years of age, should lead the first party of salvationists to Paris. So Mrs. Booth sat and sewed on the flag which she would publicly hand to her daughter in St. James's Hall, Regent Street, London, on February 4th, 1881. All Mrs. Booth's passionate love for her daughter went into the making of that flag; blue border round a deep crimson centrepiece; right in the middle a yellow sun. With glowing faith the mother pressed her needle on its task and as she sewed she prayed: prayed for her daughter, for courage, endurance and victory, prayed for France that that lovely land might not despise the young and ardent life placed at its service in the name of Christ. Praying and stitching, stitching and praying, so the flag was made.

But even in that hour of bold and glorious enterprise — surely God-directed — a human mistake crept in. Life is like that! Divine omnipotence is linked with the frail and often faulty human element. God and man . . . God and woman . . . What a partnership! Yet it succeeds. And human mistakes are swallowed up by the divine intention.

Katie knew only school French, so when her mother had sewn the flag and there only remained the motto 'Blood and Fire' to be added in red lettering within the yellow sun, she made her suggestion and the flag appeared with the device strange to French eyes, DU SANG ET DU FEU (some blood and some fire). On later flags it was corrected to SANG ET FEU.

In March 1881 the first Salvation Army meeting in France was held in a small hall in the populous and notorious Belleville district of Paris. With Katie Booth were two other young women officers: three young Englishwomen, speaking broken French with a strong accent, attempting to gain a foothold in elegant Paris!

Before long the roughest elements of the city crowded into the little hall and it was almost impossible for the salvationists to be heard, let alone for their message to be accepted. The police closed the hall for six weeks on account of the near-riots.

Poor Katie! In England, since her teens she had conducted evangelistic campaigns, preaching at times to several thousand. In France it seemed that her way was blocked, her efforts useless. But she was not going to give in! To her quivering heart she whispered, 'You may suffer, you may bleed, you may break . . . but you shall go on!'

One of the tormentors in the re-started meetings was a huge woman glorying in the nickname of 'the devil's wife'. Arms akimbo, sleeves rolled up to show her swelling muscles, she used to plant herself in the centre of the hall and mock all that was said and done.

The first real victory was as unexpected as decisive. One night some of the audience got up to dance. Jumping on a form, Katie cried out, 'Friends, I'll give you twenty minutes to dance, if you will then give me twenty minutes to speak.' A tall young workman agreed to see fair play and after twenty minutes of dancing, he stopped the excited couples and for a whole hour and twenty minutes the salvationist pleaded with them about their souls' salvation.

After the meeting the same young workman remained behind to reveal that his wife was in an asylum and that after the death of his little son he had gone to the devil. Katie prayed with him, her first soul on French soil!

Other conversions followed. The young and spirited leader now had troops behind her, troops who gave her the title of maréchale (marshal) which she bore proudly for many fruitful years.

But we have not yet finished with 'the devil's wife'. One night in the meeting a young lout used a bad word to the Maréchale and immediately 'the devil's wife' gave him a blow which nearly felled him. From that moment this amazon became Katie's bodyguard.

Katie Booth not only preached in the evenings, pouring out her heart in what was now good French, but afterwards she also visited the cafés to sell the Army paper and talk to anyone she could contact. One night she visited Café de l'Enfer (hell). It was decorated with skeletons peeping out of coffins and with grinning devils adorning the walls. She sang and spoke and as she slipped away she whispered to a young girl, 'You should not be here.' 'But who will give me a bed?' queried the girl. 'I will,' was the immediate reply, and taking her arm the Maréchale whisked her away and hailed a passing cab. At home she found the girl had noble blood in her veins and a great longing in her heart for a better life. Finally they prayed together, the girl committing herself to God. Later Katie found her protégée a position in an American college.

The rough, stormy beginnings in France, so tempestuous that they had brought the young leader to say with tight lips, 'If I cannot save France, I can at least die for it', gradually changed to a climate of acceptance. There were one hundred converts in the first twelve months, five hundred in the second year, many of them becoming salvation soldiers and some of them officers. The work was well established and has continued unabated for over ninety years.

* * *

Another story brings us nearer to our own days. Olive Gill, encouraged by her officer-parents, preached the Sunday-night sermon at Barnsley in 1912, just before her fourteenth birthday. Diminutive of stature and round of face, she looked younger than her age, but for all that she made a powerful impression as the dark eyes flashed in the small features. Her voice was clear and persuasive, carrying well without modern amplifying aids. The fervour was unmistakably sincere. There were decisions for Christ that evening.

It was an innovation which was warmly welcomed, for the bright-faced, intelligent girl was known as a staunch salvationist, an energetic worker and a good sport. Her youth, her ardour, her absorption with the theme of redemption through Jesus Christ left the audience with a desire to hear her more often. There were many enquiries, 'When is Olive going to speak again?' Again and yet again she took a responsible part in meeting-leadership and soon there came requests for her services from chapels and churches in the area. It was rather a shock for her to see herself billed as 'the girl preacher' on church announcement boards.

Olive was not the brash self-confident type. The publicity was distasteful to her, yet her sense of the duty and privilege of preaching the gospel wherever opportunity was given was powerful enough to urge her on. Four years passed, years of schooling and, later, work, but still she accepted as many calls as possible to platform or pulpit. In 1916 she trained as a Salvation Army officer and for a few years continued her evangelical ministry until her marriage.

As Mrs. Commissioner Holbrook she is in 1973 still sought after as a speaker, not only for Women's Fellowships, where she excels, but also — surprisingly, in view of her age — in youth squashes. Her good humour, clear diction, captivating illustrations and mastery of speaking technique are the outward aids: her deeply dedicated heart still supplies the motive force. As an Army writer she has made her mark also and her poems and thoughtful articles are eagerly welcomed.

CHAPTER THREE

Bonnets ... and much more

WHEN the Christian Mission was re-christened The Salvation Army in 1878 it was a logical step to adopt uniform for the officers and soldiers of the new Army, both men and women.

The bonnet has become a world symbol of service for Christ under the Army flag. It has outlived both scorn and caricature. In early days it was spat upon, smothered with bad eggs, and dented with stones hurled by savage antagonists of the new movement. But it has triumphantly recuperated from every attack.

Wearing their bonnets, the early women salvationists visited bars and houses of ill-fame with the message of salvation through Christ. In her bonnet the timid Army captain dared to go down streets where even a policeman would not go alone.

The Army bonnet was born in 1880 when the first young women ever to be called cadets arrived at the Training Home in Hackney, London. Each had made a praiseworthy though highly individual attempt at 'uniform' but the general effect was anything but acceptable. It was realised that a definite model must be introduced. Several bonnet shapes in black straw were tried on by Mrs. Catherine Booth and her daughter Emma. Their requirements were that it should be 'cheap, strong and large enough to protect the head of the wearer from cold, as well as from brickbats and other missiles'.

The first model favoured by Mrs. Booth was rejected by Miss Emma on the grounds that the women cadets would look like workhouse inmates! Finally a shape was chosen, and a cadet who was a milliner was instructed to trim it with black silk, pleated inside the brim, with long black ribbons to tie under the chin. Sufficient of these bonnets were prepared for all the cadets and, one long-awaited day, twenty-five young women marched for the first time in Army bonnets. For the sake of truth it must be admitted that some of the girls were human enough to object to wearing 'such old-fashioned bonnets', while all the rest of womenkind wore gay flower-trimmed headgear. It is recorded that the milliner cadet herself, once she was safely away from London, added a touch of white ruching inside her bonnet-brim to improve its appearance.

The Army bonnet has passed through a number of phases since that time. It has been large and weighty — facetiously referred to as a coal-scuttle; the black silk has given way to navy blue; the ruching inside the front edge has been replaced by plain silk; the long wide ribbons which used to flap in the wind have changed to a neat bow and chin-strap; and the bonnet itself has shrunk to the smallest possible dimensions. Since 1884 it bears a red Salvation Army band tucked into its pleated trimming.

With the modern open-necked uniforms, the bonnet can be exchanged for a smart little hat with a badge in front, but many love the traditional bonnet and will always give it preference.

Sweaters and T-shirts with lettering are all the rage our days but so they were a hundred years ago in Salvation Army circles. The writer has an old photo of her mother, the young and serious face framed in an Army bonnet rising to rather a high peak in the centre front. The photo is sepia but the jersey was undoubtedly dark crimson. Across the chest in large letters worked in cross-stitch are the words, in Swedish, JESUS LOVES YOU. Other salvationists satisfied themselves with the single word JESUS. A few chose HALLELUJAH as expressing their sentiments. Of one man — surely of an original turn of mind — it is recorded that he wore SAVED BY GRACE on the front of his jersey and READ THE WAR CRY on the back.

With bonnets for women and caps for men, both with the familiar red lettered band, the next step was to determine some kind of suit or costume to accompany them. Old advertisements in the *War Cry*, the Army's weekly periodical, show a tall, waisted female with a three-quarter length jacket fastened by eighteen small buttons. An ample flowing skirt reaches the ground, and is edged with Russian braid to combat wear and tear as the hem of the skirt sweeps the floor. This uniform is announced as a marvel of cheapness in two qualities, 17/6d and 22/6d, less one shilling in the pound discount, and with an extra charge of one shilling for made to measure. It is guaranteed that the material WILL NOT FADE but a cheaper stuff that WILL FADE (in large letters) can also be obtained. Such honest advertising is surely rare.

The same advertisement bears a notice about the dressing department of The Salvation Army which is

under the experienced and efficient direction of a well-known staff officer. She is well-saved, has a definite daily salvation, knows what lasses need and can be trusted to supply and interpret the wants of her fellow-warriors.

Bonnet and uniform! What else does a woman salvationist need? She needs her Bible, the Word of God, from which to preach and to seek guidance for herself. She needs a flag to follow, the red-yellow-blue flag which unites salvationists the world over. It is the symbol of their faith.

The crimson ground is the message of hope that 'the blood of Jesus Christ, God's Son, cleanseth from all sin'. The blue and yellow represent the two aspects of holiness: blue, the Old Testament colour for purity, and yellow, the fire of the Holy Spirit giving power for witness and service. The first Army flag was presented to Coventry corps by Catherine Booth in 1879.

In early days the 'Blood and Fire flag', as it is affectionately called, was often the scorn of its enemies and the target of their assaults. When it was taken out on the march in Folkestone for the first time, salvationists had to form a bodyguard round the colour-sergeant to protect him. To reach the hall they had to pass through a long railway tunnel. A hooligan put out the only street lamp in the archway as a signal for attacking the march. As the group of men and women re-formed into procession on emerging from the tunnel, they found to their dismay that the colour-sergeant carried only a pole. The flag was missing! How the roughs jeered! A saddened group marched to the hall lamenting their lost banner. As they filed dispiritedly into the hall, they saw standing on the platform a little asthmatical old clergyman waving the missing flag! As he followed the Army march through the tunnel, he heard the roughs plotting to steal the flag; so in the darkness he crept up and snatched it himself, hiding it under his coat. Then, panting and breathless, he had taken a short cut to the hall to hand back the treasured banner.

Just before the revolution which forced The Salvation Army out of Russia after ten years' involvement, a young man student was converted. One night when he went as usual to the hall in Moscow, he found it closed and a military officer informed him that The Salvation Army had been dissolved. All Army belongings had been confiscated or destroyed except 'an old floor-cloth', which happened to be the flag! The women officers had been sent to prison, but some salvationists got possession of the flag and began secret meetings out in the forest. After a few weeks a girl lieutenant was released from prison, and in a glade of the pine forest she accepted the young convert as a Salvation Army soldier under the folds of the so-called 'floor-cloth', the treasured Army flag.

The young man later escaped from Russia with his mother and found shelter in France where he became a Salvation Army officer.

*   *   *

Away in Japan at the turn of the century a young educated woman from an ancient Samurai family came into touch with The Salvation Army in Tokyo. Following the family tradition of service to those in need, Kieko looked for some sphere where her spare time could be employed. Her brother was in the imperial navy, later rising to the rank of admiral, and she knew from him how temptations awaited the young naval ratings in port. If she could only start something to keep them from immoral enticements! Perhaps a reading room, or a club? When her teaching-duties at school were over she sought out prominent men, asking if her leisure hours could not be used for some purpose. In frank and kindly manner she was told that it would be better for her to get married, and look after her own home and children, than to get embroiled in social problems.

A friend took her to some Salvation Army meetings but Kieko was appalled by what she heard and saw. The two English missionaries did their utmost with the language, but their utter lack of elementary Japanese etiquette was shocking. Finding out where they lived, Kieko called on them and offered to give them language lessons and at the same time instruct them in necessary public etiquette. They welcomed her gracious gesture with relief and in exchange asked a young Japanese captain, Gunpei Yamamuro, to explain Army terms and methods to her. This he did so wholeheartedly that he fell in love with Kieko and later married her.

When Mrs. Kieko Yamamuro became a Salvation Army officer, she sought to give devoted service in every possible way, with two reservations. She was not willing to march through the streets, nor would she play a tambourine. The only women in Japan who performed on instruments were geisha girls, generally of questionable character.

The fact that she hid these two reservations in her heart troubled gentle, sincere Kieko. She wanted to be 'all out' for God, as her husband so often exhorted his people to be. In a watch-night service she determined to surrender her pride. The next march saw Kieko Yamamuro with radiant face playing a tambourine and singing joyfully. She had conquered herself! It was the first of many times when she would force herself to do even an unpleasant duty with a smile, because she did it for God.

One bitterly cold day she stood in the open-air service with chapped and bleeding hands, playing her tambourine to the songs. Later she noticed that it was stained with her blood. The price of sacrifice!

In the year 1900 The Salvation Army started its crusade for the liberation of prostitutes in Japan. Prostitution was then regarded as inevitable, and each city and town had its licensed quarters. Girls from poor families were sold to the brothels in times of flood, famine or earthquake because money was scarce. There they lived like trapped birds in cages. Any girl who escaped was hunted down by the police who restored her to her 'owners'. It was open and unashamed slavery to a life of vice, as long as the girls had their health. When they were old or sick they could be thrown out. Many times they chose suicide to end their lives.

Careful preparations were made for the Army's attack on the evil in the notorious Yoshiwara district of Tokyo. A special issue of the Japanese *War Cry* was prepared, inviting girls who longed for liberty to contact the Army. After a whole night of prayer, with tense and determined faces, the handful of salvationists marched with music and singing right into the heart of the licensed district, distributing the *War Cry* with its flaming message of rescue to the girls.

The brothel-keepers did not take this attack on their territory without a spirited response. The salvationists were mobbed and beaten and emerged with torn uniforms, bleeding faces, broken drums and smashed instruments.

Next night two terrified girls escaped in their night-clothes and knocked desperately on the headquarters' door. They were admitted and hidden. Letters came from others, begging for help to obtain their release. The situation looked ugly for the salvationists, who had been warned on pain of death never to set foot in the Yoshiwara district again. Assistance came from an unexpected quarter. The daily press became alarmed at foreigners being attacked in the streets, and shame was voiced that the Japanese nation should carry the slur of open prostitution on its name. Public opinion ran so high that the Emperor signed an ordinance stating that any girl who wished to leave a brothel was free to go when she liked, by filling in a notice of cessation. Within a year twelve thousand girls gained their liberty.

The Army equipped a home to receive girls leaving brothels

and Kieko Yamamuro was placed in charge. She begged clothing for the girls, who had only what they wore. She taught them cooking, sewing and housework. If she saw that they were sick, she sent them off to the hospital. For some she found situations where they could earn a respectable living until they married. Kieko knew that moral uplift was not enough. She taught them to believe in God, and to pray. She explained Bible stories to them, for they were hearing them for the first time.

To cope with all the demands of the receiving home and her own growing family placed great strain on Kieko. She and her husband had only one small room where they lived, and they shared meals with the girls of the home. Finally the responsibility grew too great, and Kieko was asked instead to take charge of a girls' home, while her husband continued as the editor of the *War Cry*.

The girls arriving at the new home had been brought in from a famine area. Starved, ill-clad, wandering from village to village with their families in search of food, there was every risk that they would be sold secretly as prostitutes. Kieko mothered them from the rich stores of her love and taught them the simple tasks of a home so that they could take situations as servants. This would ensure them food and a roof over their heads.

The greatest task which Kieko would do for her homeland still lay ahead. It was something quite contrary to her quiet, retiring disposition. It was another unpleasant task which she would do with a smile because it was for God and the people. The Army's small general hospital was over-filled, the greatest number of cases being those of tuberculosis. A sanatorium was obviously needed, but there was no money. After much prayer she decided to offer to collect the large sum required.

Collecting money was — and is — the bugbear of most officers, and costs them the greatest self-discipline. Yet it is necessary, for without the financial help the public gives, the Army could not continue its service for others.

Kieko grappled with her nervousness. Too reserved to speak to another person of what was in her thoughts, she nevertheless committed her feelings to her diary. In that way we can peep into the depths of her soul on this matter.

It seems too adventurous perhaps, but God is able. I have no one save the Holy Ghost to rely upon. My weak health and lack of ability seem to deny me success, but when I am weak, God is strong. Depending upon Him alone, I go forward to establish the Sanatorium. To be with the children makes me happy and perhaps some will call me neglectful of my duty as a mother. But though my eyes are wet with tears, I must go forward. O Lord, fill me with the Holy Ghost. Give me power to move the people. Amen.

Kieko next made out a list of a thousand leading people of Tokyo and went from office to office, from home to home, pleading and explaining, asking for money for the project. When the list was nearly at an end, she stopped to count the money. She had only about one-third of what was required! To God she went in prayer and another idea grew. With her skilful fingers she traced the characters of a touching appeal, not too long, not too short; well-displayed and artistic. Then she made many copies. It took time, but she forced herself to sit at the task. Armed with these she visited noble ladies, prevailed upon twenty-seven of them to sign a copy and to present it to their friends. In this way the circle of her influence spread. God honoured the brave effort and the remainder of the money was forthcoming.

It was Kieko Yamamuro's last great service for the Army in

her homeland. At the birth of her fourth son she died, only forty-two years of age. As her life ebbed away she struggled to give a last message to her husband and children. It was the simple phrase, 'God first'.

A modern, well-equipped children's home in Japan was re-opened in 1970 as a memorial to this fine Christlike woman. It bears her name, the Kieko Children's Home.

*   *   *

No Salvation Army officer draws more than an allowance which is allocated according to years of service and rank. The nurses, teachers, writers, composers, accountants, architects, all give to the utmost of their capabilities without extra remuneration. It is a simple philosophy. All one's gifts are dedicated to serve God and mankind under the Army flag, and the glory and honour of such service lies in the fact that the balance between giving and getting is always weighted on the heavenly side. As Mildred Duff once charged young officers, 'Be sure you always give more to the Army than you ever receive from it. In that way your service will be blessed and honoured by God.'

As a world-wide organisation, The Salvation Army uses many languages to get across the message of salvation, while English remains the medium of correspondence between the various countries. Army comradeship must be among the richest in the world, for the one flag unites men and women of all nations, and the uniform does away with the need for personal presentation.

Many officers are linguists of considerable merit, having learned in the hard field of experience. A few specialise in platform translation which is much more difficult than its written counterpart. Sentence-by-sentence interpretation is a made-to-measure solution to the problem of giving a visiting leader contact with a congregation whose language he does not know. Because of the Army's internationalism this has been developed to a fine art.

Some women officers have made a name for themselves as efficient and reliable platform translators. One very experienced woman — a veteran in the art – is Colonel Hildegard Bleick of Germany. Her erect commanding figure with its pleasant attractive face has stood side by side with many a visiting leader. It requires not only intelligence and quick wits but also a good measure of humility to be but a channel and in no way the author of what is said. Hildegard Bleick has high qualities of her own which make her very acceptable as a speaker.

As a blonde and blue-eyed girl, Hildegard did not think much of religion. She attended a Bible study circle in the home of a school teacher for three years, but without enjoying it. Then she started dancing-lessons at the opera in Berlin, and rhythm got into her blood. She was frank with her teacher. She would not be attending Bible study any more as she found it 'too pious'.

A few months later a friend told her excitedly one morning, 'You should have been with us last night. We had a thrilling time. We went to The Salvation Army! It was a good thing that there were several of us, for they hypnotise people to make them go forward to the Penitent Form.'

Hildegard made her friend promise to take her next evening. The two girls giggled now and then but they were gripped by the sincerity of the testimonies. They were soon regular attenders at the meetings. When the question of getting converted posed itself to Hildegard's mind, she silenced it hurriedly with the flat statement, 'You can't! If you get converted you're finished with dancing and you know you *must* dance.'

Her parents were very angry when they learned she was attending Army meetings, and they gave her a rough time. One evening early in 1921 when Hildegard was sixteen years old, she went forward to the Penitent Form and after a prolonged struggle surrendered to God, giving Him first place in her life. After that, dancing did not seem to matter, but persecution at home increased. For four years the girl did not hear a single kind word from her parents. They were church people and bitterly opposed their daughter's interest in The Salvation Army. While going home from each meeting, Hildegard knew that she would be met with angry reproaches. Once her mother sent someone to fetch her out of a meeting by force. It was a humiliating scene.

What changed the situation with the parents was their daughter's decision to take matters into her own hands. She would leave home, going to Hungary to help the newly-appointed Army leaders there. The wife was a cripple and although Hildegard Bleick was no born housewife, she could at least peel potatoes and boil an egg. At any rate, she would try to make herself useful. Surprised at the sudden turn of events, her father capitulated to the extent of buying his daughter a uniform, on the understanding that she would not wear it until the morning of her departure for Budapest. Hildegard was away a whole year and her absence changed the home atmosphere. 'I want my girl back,' wrote her father, her mother attended some evangelical meetings, and became an active Christian.

Back in Berlin, Hildegard completed her training as a Salvation Army officer and was sent once more to Hungary. She was to live in the home of an English salvationist-leader, and it was there that she improved her schoolgirl-English. Her first platform-translating assignments were from English to Hungarian — both of them acquired languages not yet quite perfect.

Later a rather comic situation developed when she was translating sentence by sentence from German to Hungarian. Dramatically describing a dream, the woman speaker continued, 'and suddenly an angel stood by my bedside'. Poor Hildegard in her nervousness mixed up two words which are very alike in Hungarian, and announced, 'and suddenly an Englishman stood by my bedside'. The speaker could not understand the sudden burst of laughter in what was intended to be a solemn moment. With red face Hildegard had to explain her mistake and rectify it.

Five years of service in Czechoslovakia followed the Hungarian period. The meetings in Prague were always very lively as the Czech salvationists were enthusiastic. Crowds flocked to the meetings. By now Hildegard Bleick had five languages at her command: German, English, Hungarian, Czech, and a good knowledge of French from her high-school days when her favourite subject was languages.

Later years were spent in her homeland Germany in training-work. She loved the quiet of the lecture-hall when she stood before young men and women who had dedicated their lives to God's cause under the Army flag. She watched the flickers of emotion on their faces, sensed how they reacted to challenge, how earnestly they imbibed Bible knowledge and grappled with doctrine, with what doggedness they tried to learn all the intricacies of Salvation Army regulations. In a sense it was the fulfilment of her girlhood's dream of being a teacher. She had become a teacher-evangelist. That was even better.

Colonel Hildegard Bleick has translated for most Army leaders visiting Germany, so she has become an expert. Her ability even attracted the attention of a British military general who was chairing a lecture given by General Orsborn of The Salvation Army. After hearing the efficient and rapid translating, the military man leaned over to the salvationist-general. 'I'd like to have that lady as translator on my staff.' General Orsborn replied, 'Sorry, sir. She belongs to us and we need her.'

When Commissioner Catherine Bramwell-Booth visited Berlin in her capacity as international secretary she always used Colonel Bleick as her translator.

The Commissioner knew some German but not enough to be free in her addresses. Once while the translating was proceeding, Commissioner Catherine turned to her translator and said *in German*, 'I didn't say that. These interpreters think they can do what they like!'

Flushing with embarrassment Colonel Bleick replied, 'I gave the sense of what you said, even if I used other words.'

Commissioner Catherine, patting her arm, smiled at her, adding, 'Dear Bleick, don't you know that the audience like nothing better than the two on the platform getting across each other?' She had staged the incident just to increase their concentration. With an amused laugh, the congregation settled down once again to listening, by now very wide awake.

In 1968 Colonel Bleick retired officially but she still continues translating in public. She is also in charge of the Army's Missing Persons' Bureau and the Education Department — a fully active retirement for a charming and efficient officer who still retains her youthful enthusiasm, her twinkling eyes and ready laugh witnessing to her happy Christianity and her positive approach to life.

CHAPTER FOUR

The Unconventional Approach

How far should the unconventional be used in God's service — doing something spectacular at an unexpected place and time, simply to make people stop and think, and perhaps stay to pray? Early salvationists were not pious devotees appearing in decorous dress only at the appointed hour of worship. They were militants for God and His Kingdom. 'Jesus shall conquer' was their battle cry and in the face of antagonism or apathy they threw themselves upon the heart of God in pleading, prevailing prayer.

Army soldiers of bygone days were more uninhibited than now, but it would be wrong to suppose that it was merely sensationalism. Many daring stunts took place after a night of prayer, born of an agonised longing to see people saved.

Take Happy Eliza. Flamboyant posters had announced the new assistant in Marylebone as 'Happy Eliza' instead of the more sober 'Lieutenant Eliza Haynes'. She accompanied an officer who had been successful at previous places, and together the two were a striking and resourceful pair. But the district did not react to their presence. Eliza decided to live up to her new title.

She painted the words 'Happy Eliza' on long ribbons which she fastened to her head; then with her loose hair flying in the wind (she was only a youngster) she ran up and down the backstreets shouting invitations to the meetings. Crowds began to fill the hall. But that is only the outside story. The inside story is that it was from a half-night of prayer that the girl had gone on her wild race through the streets.

Happy Eliza played the fiddle and was soon leading the singing on the marches by waving her bow and sometimes — in the exuberance of the moment — the fiddle itself. A contemporary sketch shows her at Marylebone sitting beside the driver on the front of a horse-drawn cab, fiddle and bow waving, with a drummer in uniform on the roof thumping out rhythm, and other salvationists inside throwing out handbills through the open windows.

Three thousand people filled the theatre for the first meeting in Marylebone on Sunday, April 4th, 1880. Happy Eliza became a household word throughout England. Songs about her were sung in music-halls, and dolls, toys and sweets were named after her. Grimy-faced urchins could ask in the sweet shops for 'an a'porth o' 'appy 'Lizas', and get them too.

*   *   *

Jeanie Budge had generations of good Scotch blood in her veins, so that when she gave herself to God and pledged to serve Him, she meant it. She was only fifteen, and the thought of having to tell her strict and rather narrow-minded mother of her decision filled her with apprehension, without in any way damping her intention. The scene at her home in Scotland was even more painful than she had anticipated.

In being saved, Jeanie realised that she must renounce the world and all vanity. Vanity for her consisted of her brooch, bracelet and a feather in her straw hat. Arriving home, she walked straight to the kitchen where a glowing fire lit the darkness. Pulling off brooch and bracelet and tearing the feather from her hat, she cast them into the flames. Then she turned to face her mother and told her about her conversion.

Mrs. Budge, irate at the news that her Jeanie had knelt in public at the Army's Penitent Form and intended to join that strange sect, gave her a choice: to renounce the Army or to leave home at once, and for ever. Harsh words to a young girl! But the daughter was fashioned from the same stern flint as the mother. Both were unwavering. Jeanie made her decision. Out into the night she went, dressed as she had come home, barring the finery, and with nothing else. It was many years before she entered her home again.

She went straight to friends she had met at the Army and they took her in for the time being. It was imperative that she should find some work at once, so she lengthened her skirts, rolled her plait up into a bun and applied to be a ward maid at the local hospital. She was taken on immediately without any question of age, so both lodging and a meagre wage were assured.

Jeanie had to pray over every penny she spent, for now she must be self-supporting. The following year she applied to be trained as an officer, but was considered to young. At seventeen she tried again with the same result. At eighteen she was accepted as a cadet. She had been faithful to God, but in spite of her efforts at a reconciliation at home, her mother remained obdurate and refused to meet her. It was a great sorrow to Jeanie.

Once out in the thick of God's battlefield, Captain Jeanie Budge showed her mettle. In one corps no one responded to her invitation to meetings or opened the door when she visited the homes. What could she do to break down this indifference? Jeanie did what many before and after her have done. She sought God in prayer and wrestled before Him a whole night, pleading for the souls of the careless people of that town. Through prayer came courage and faith, and finally a plan of action.

Next day was market day. Crowds would be assembling round the stalls on the square. Jeanie waited until business was brisk, then she donned a tall paper hat in vivid colours and marched round and round in ever narrowing circles in complete silence. Folk stopped and stared, whispering 'She's gone daft.' Jeanie took no notice. Round and round she continued until people began to press in upon her as the circle grew smaller. Then she stopped and spoke out, lashing them with her Scottish tongue. Even a strong man quails before sanctified fury! In blazing terms she flailed them, charging them with neglect of the claims of God, and with living selfish, careless lives with no thought for eternity. Finally — and her eyes flashed as she said it — came her last volley: 'You will only listen to me when I wear a paper hat and act the fool. Well, I'm willing to be a fool for Christ.' With a contemptuous gesture she flung the paper hat from her head. 'Tonight I shall preach in the Army hall. I shall expect you all to be there.' Turning on her heel she marched home, red patches flaming on her cheeks.

That night the hall was full and a number of people were saved. From then on Jeanie Budge had evidence that God was with her, blessing her service. So successful did she become that she was appointed in the 1920s to train cadets in field tactics. The successive groups of young women who came under her influence during those years remember her as a firebrand for God. Stern but just, she demanded high standards. That alone would have made its mark on young lives, but what made the greatest impression was what she was in herself, her passion for God and His cause, her continuous prayer-life under the duties of the day, her inflexible adhesion to duty and her love for souls.

From 1928 on Lt.-Colonel Jeanie Budge was engaged in the social services in her home town, Glasgow. Shrewd and devoted as a leader, she still retained her high standards of duty, these leading her to an over-spending of her energies. Some years of ill-health in retirement preceded her death in 1939.

*   *   *

The title of 'Java's one-armed angel' might lead to considerable speculation. It was given to Brigadier Esther Pettersson after a life-time of service, much of it among lepers.

As a teenage salvationist in her homeland, Sweden, Esther had a vision of herself working among lepers. Even in her vision she sensed a numbing feeling of isolation and loneliness. Then she felt God's hand on her shoulder and His voice said, 'You see what it costs? Are you willing?' The answer came after long hesitation. It was a whispered 'Yes'.

In 1912 when Esther arrived at her first appointment as a Salvation Army officer in a leper colony in Indonesia she was astounded to recognise the scene of her vision: the surrounding jungle, the white huts, the narrow paths which led to the world outside overgrown with grass, for they were seldom used.

During the first nine years of her service Esther showed astonishing ability to adapt, as well as courage and initiative. She learnt to bandage, feed and dress the patients; she learnt, too, the language so that she could soon lead daily prayers or speak in the Sunday services. She gloried in her life-work, but a cruel set-back awaited her. The authorities decreed that only those with full nursing qualifications could continue to serve the patients. Esther had the practice but not the theory!

Homeland furlough was overdue. She made her plans. A

brief visit to Sweden was all she allowed herself, then she started nursing studies in Holland. She was a quick and industrious pupil but shortly before the final examination she was involved in a train disaster. Her right arm was crushed and had to be amputated. Esther was dogged by nature and she also had a divine call to leper work. With assiduous practice she trained her left hand and passed the examinations, receiving her diploma. The doctors were so impressed by her resolute courage that they themselves paid for an artificial arm for her and allocated a nurse to teach her to use it as quickly as possible.

So the one-armed nurse came back to Java and once more entered whole-heartedly into service for lepers, abandoned children, and anyone who needed help. Her optimistic disposition, her shining faith in God, and her astounding capacity for work impressed everyone. Then came the Second World War and three years of internment.

Esther reported to the Japanese camp commandant and asked for permission to act as nurse to her fellow-internees. Afterwards one of them said to a journalist, 'That one-armed Swedish woman did more than ten healthy men.' The camp officials were so impressed by her courageous self-denying service in the tragic years that followed that Esther was offered her liberty. This she refused, choosing rather to suffer with the internees where her services were so much needed. There was much illness, few medicines, and so little food that any snakes, rats or snails the prisoners could find were a welcome addition to the cooking pot!

Twenty-nine years of her life Esther Pettersson gave to the suffering in Indonesia. It is no wonder that she was affectionately called 'Java's one-armed angel'.

*　　　*　　　*

Emmy van Hoogstraten, a qualified Dutch nurse, was trained in London in 1932 as a Salvation Army officer, and was sent to help in the former Belgian Congo, now Zaïre. When the revolution broke out she was working in Stanleyville and was ordered to evacuate with other missionaries and Europeans. But Emmy was a strong and dedicated personality with intrepid courage in her make-up. When the plane carrying the missionaries touched down in Usumbura, Ruanda-Urundi, she stepped off. She had decided to stay in Africa!

To employ her time usefully she undertook Bible translations until she could return to the Congo. Hearing in September 1960 that all was quiet in Stanleyville, she intended to return but received a message asking her to go instead to Elizabethville. There was a plane leaving the next day.

In the morning there was a violent earthquake followed by a series of tremors. The asphalted roads rose and fell like waves on a sea and great rifts appeared. The grinding, roaring noise from within the earth was terrifying. People rushed into the streets as their houses began to collapse. Brigadier van Hoogstraten spent the day and night in the Consul's home near to the airport, alert all the time for further quakes. Next morning, despite continual slight tremors, the plane was able to take off.

Elizabethville was hardly safer than Usumbura. There were no earthquakes, true, but there was war. Emmy found that one of her first duties was to visit wounded soldiers in the city's four hospitals. All Protestant and Roman Catholic padres had been sent back to Europe; so Emmy became spiritual adviser and confidante to many hundreds of men. She wrote letters for them, brought them gifts of fruit and tinned milk which she begged from the authorities, and had the joy of giving out gospel portions which were eagerly accepted. Some men asked for Bibles and she managed to obtain and distribute one hundred and twenty Bibles in twelve different languages.

Five times Emmy came under fire and twice her car was pierced by bullets. Not only her days were filled with danger, but also her nights. There was always shooting in the nearby Baluba Camp with its thirty-five thousand inmates. The men indulged in strong drink and took African opium, then broke out of camp to murder and steal. Many were cannibals and there were lurid stories of people being killed and eaten. In her visits to hospitals Emmy saw many badly mutilated people, and heard that parts of their bodies had been cut off and eaten raw before their eyes!

With indomitable spirit she worked on, the only missionary left in the district. Not all her time went to the wounded and destitute. In the evenings she held meetings, gathering the salvationists of the city and imbuing them with her faith and trust in God.

In 1962, despite continued war and lack of necessities, she reported that they had had a wonderful Eastertide, with ten new salvation soldiers enrolled and a small school started. Her days settled into a more regular rhythm of relief work in the morning, and distributing food parcels in the afternoon. For the evening she added a Bible study course and music lessons to the established meeting programme, with Sunday school for the children.

She was nearing the retirement age of sixty but pleaded, 'Don't send anyone to replace me just now. I feel younger than ever! I love these people. These last weeks God has answered our prayers for souls and we have had ten decisions.'

One more year was given to Brigadier Emmy van Hoogstraten to work in her beloved Congo; then followed an overdue homeland furlough in Holland with retirement in the offing.

One who visited her in Elizabethville and saw her labour of love summed it up in the words, 'She is a very courageous soul doing a grand work alone.'

*   *   *

Another who has developed an exceptional line in her service is Major Joy Webb of the golden voice, so well known that she hardly needs an introduction. In most entertaining style she has recorded her own adventurous living in *And This is Joy.** She is often praised as a song and music writer and performer but rarely for her prose writing, which has a distinctive colourful quality. She is so natural, so vivacious, yet manages to pack a message of real worth: she *communicates.*

The child of Salvation Army officers, Joy had to share their roving life and it was twelve houses and seven schools later that she branched out on her own, needing, as she expresses it, 'a holy shove' to get her into the right groove in life. Her seventeen years as an Army officer have certainly not had anything groove-like about them. Joy is not the type to remain in any confining rut.

She was soon thrown into the hectic but happy life in a corps with all its demands — preaching, visiting, conducting dedications (christenings) and funerals, counselling and comforting. She revelled in the many-sided activities but was then drafted back to the Training College at Denmark Hill, London. Although she did not know it, this was a vital turning-point. A skiffle band started it all.

Joy had always had music and rhythm in her blood. Her father was a well-known Salvation Army drummer, not the *bang-bang* type but the dedicated artist of a thousand subtleties. Much to her delight he used to demonstrate drumming

* Hodder and Stoughton, 25p.

patterns at the dinner table, using a pair of knives on an up-turned plate and working up to such a frenzy of delirious drumming that all the utensils and cutlery within reach were soon involved. And all this while mother was waiting to serve the pudding!

When Joy took cadets out on campaign they packed an arsenal of wash-boards, bazookas and cocoa-tins filled with dried peas to give plenty of background noise, and once hit the headlines of a Midland daily with their skiffle performance.

More was to come. The electric guitar made its appearance. Fredrick Coutts, newly elected General of The Salvation Army, expressed the hope that the movement might show a more modern approach to its task of evangelising, and even mentioned the possibility of taking the gospel message to coffee-bars, with the help of electric guitars. He little knew at the time what an amazing effect those simple words would have.

There were even cartoons in the press, and a frenzied hunt for Army people who could and would play and sing. Joy was right in the centre of the electrical guitar storm and was launched on a new phase in her career.

The Joystrings were formed and functioned for five hectic years, trying to meet some of the many requests for their participation. The Blue Angel Club, the steps of St. Paul's cathedral, schools, colleges, prisons, London's Playboy Club, and many churches, chapels and Army halls presented them with critical or captivated crowds — more often a mixture of both! For it was not all plain sailing for the Joystrings. Within the Army, as in other religious circles, there was considerable criticism of this 'demeaning' of the gospel message. One minister felt his church had been 'desecrated' by the visit of the group.

But Joy won through — against both adverse officialdom and private verbal attacks. The pressing need for suitable songs forced her into writing her own and she has composed well over a hundred songs, all with that gripping appeal to the heart which characterises her work.

The Joystrings are now disbanded but the Joyfolk often appear with Joy Webb. She has visited almost all European lands where the Army operates and has also done extensive tours taking her as far as Australia and New Zealand, Canada and the United States, Hong Kong, Singapore and the Philippines. Her task is to encourage other Army rhythm groups, and her frank but friendly comments have changed many a rough-and-ready bunch of howlers and yowlers into a well-trimmed disciplined ensemble.

One of the highlights of one of her tours was the massive 'Palaver '71' build-up in Utrecht, Holland. This gigantic venture of faith, sponsored by the European and Dutch Bible Societies and given solid backing by the Dutch Government, gathered together a crowd of twenty-two thousand students from neighbouring lands. It was a magnificent attempt to bring the Bible and its standards right on to the contemporary scene. Joy and her group had been given the task of starting off the Reli-Pop Festival with a thirty-minute performance. It was a big event and there was some excuse for initial nervousness, but towards the end of the half-hour the audience was standing on the seats, clapping rhythmically in overhead beat and singing with all stops pulled out. A tremendous occasion!

The name of Joy Webb alerts all the mass-media folk, and wherever she goes she has to face a blizzard of camera flashes and television crews, with microphones everywhere. On arrival in Hong Kong she went through the customary press and television barrage and was then whisked off to tape a thirty-minute programme of religious music, after which she met the nine hundred students in the Army's school and was the guest-speaker at the Kowloon Rotary Club — all in a morning's work. She follows a gruelling programme, but manages to come through smiling and serene.

In Australia in 1972 she recorded a disc of four of her songs, the proceeds of sales to go to the Joy Webb Music Scholarship to help young Australian salvationists further in their musical studies. Some of her most touching moments are not when she stands on the stage singing to thousands, but when in private conversation she is able to help someone to a living faith in Christ. After youth meetings in Brisbane, Joy received a tele-phone call from a young woman lecturer in psychiatry who said that she had been thinking over the message given in word and song, adding, 'I need to move into this new dimension, but it will mean a radical change in my way of living. Do you really believe that this can happen to a human being?' Joy could assure her definitely that she did. Quick as a flash came the request, 'Will you pray with me then, over the phone?' So over the phone the prayer was said and contact made with God.

Perhaps the most original attempt to advertise Joy Webb's visit was made in Auckland, New Zealand. Five thousand colourful carrier bags were sold with the words *This is Joy* printed in large letters over them. Everybody seemed to carry one and this certainly highlighted Christ's promise of joy to His disciples — the central theme of the gatherings. Young New Zealanders flocked to hear Joy and listened with sustained attention. Perhaps the greatest moment of spiritual intensity was when she sang slowly to her own guitar accompaniment, the quiet song 'Have faith in God'. One by one, thoughtfully and deliberately, lads and girls rose from their places and made their way to the front to surrender their lives to God, their footsteps in no way disturbing the golden voice that sang them into the Kingdom of Heaven.

In Wellington a girl drug addict came to stand at the front with Joy in response to her appeal. Her restless eyes were full of fear. 'Help me,' she whispered, 'help me.' Joy prayed with her, then slipped a little badge from her uniform and pressed it into the girl's hand as a token that she would remember her before God. Later came a letter from the girl to say that she was climbing out of the pit of her addiction. Some gleam of gospel truth had got through to her. She now had a rope to hold on to.

Back in England in 1972 a full programme awaited Joy. One interesting event took her and her group to a twenty-minute 'spot' in a Sunday show at the Lyceum Ballroom, London, when ten copies of the *Living New Testament* were distributed to members of the cast of the Edwardian Variety Show. Money for these books came from the interest on a bequest to the Army many years ago, which was to be used for giving New Testaments 'to circus clowns and variety artists'. It is hoped to distribute more Testaments in the future to 'showbiz' people.

Recently Joy's portrait has been painted by Lady Sybil Richardson. She is shown sitting in almost pensive mood, striking a chord on her guitar. The portrait will be a permanent memory of a dedicated life, working through a modern medium.

CHAPTER FIVE

Behind Prison Walls

OPPOSITION to The Salvation Army has never had the power to deter it. Had the moral and spiritual fibre of early salvationists been weak, the movement would not exist today. Slander and caricature have stiffened its spine. That type of opposition is often easier to live with than the indifference which marks our own time. In Great Britain the first salvationists drew upon themselves the anger and ridicule of mobs. At Guildford in 1882 brutal attacks were made even on the women-folk. One woman was knocked down and kicked unconscious. Another was so badly injured that she died a few days later. In Worthing the woman Army leader received a death-blow from a flying stone during rioting.

The first woman officer to suffer imprisonment in Great Britain was gaoled in 1879 for three days in Pentre, Wales, for having knelt to pray in the 'road' — it was actually on a large open place. She was in frail health and died eighteen months later as a result of disease contracted in prison.

In 1885 a young lieutenant was sentenced to a month's imprisonment for singing in York market. Ironically enough, The Salvation Army had written authority from the City of York to hold meetings on that very spot! A memorial to the Home Secretary was signed by five thousand people within four days

59

and the girl was released when half her sentence had been served.

The women officers ordered to prison were usually escorted by their soldiers and even by bands. There was a kind of rejoicing in tribulation, an element of sanctified hilarity, a waving of banners and clapping of hands to enthusiastic singing before the prison door clanged shut on the new inmate. The last words ringing in her ears would be, 'We'll be praying for you!' That memory fortified her in her cell. On release after serving her sentence she would find the band waiting to escort her home with great jubilation.

This counting it all joy to suffer for righteousness' sake led a Swedish captain to send a hastily written letter to her headquarters in Stockholm: 'Hallelujah! In an hour and a half I shall be sitting in the prison cart on my way to gaol. Praise the Lord.'

The prison sentences imposed on numbers of Swedish salvationists in the 1880s were chiefly for contravention of an unjust law passed to prevent them holding meetings after darkness had fallen. The sentences could be anything up to one month. In the case of two women officers it was thirteen days in prison because they had continued their meeting thirteen minutes over the time allowed. Their appeal that they were praying with seekers at the Penitent Form during those minutes was ignored.

Switzerland has always boasted of its religious freedom but Katie Booth, the Maréchale, who stretched out her hands from France to conquer new realms, was to learn otherwise. She conducted the inaugural meeting in Geneva in December 1882 and that was the beginning of serious opposition. Rioting against the salvationists took wilder and more dangerous forms than in other lands, and scores of Army soldiers were sent to prison for trying to lead Swiss people to Christ. Eventually the Army was ordered to cease its activities and the Maréchale was expelled from Geneva in February 1883.

But Katie Booth had a strong will which was not so easily thwarted. She entered another Swiss canton but soon found herself in prison awaiting trial. A visitor discovered her planning future campaigns and not at all cast down. Patting the walls of her cell she exclaimed, 'How I love these walls. Jesus has been with me here and He fills the place with His presence.'

In 1888 a Scottish girl serving in Switzerland, Captain Charlotte Stirling, was convicted of having invited children to a meeting and written 'Are you saved?' in the snow. She was sentenced to a hundred days' imprisonment in the Castle of Chillon, the lakeside setting well known to tourists. From prison Charlotte wrote, 'I look at the waves furiously beating against the rocks beneath my cell window. The castle stands firm. So do we, founded on the Rock of Ages.'

These are old stories, of course, and Switzerland has long since opened her arms to The Salvation Army and its ministry. In 1958 – the Army's seventy-fifth anniversary in that land – the bonnet was given signal honour by being used as a coloured engraving on a postage stamp.

*　　　*　　　*

Some imprisonments were imposed not simply for preaching the gospel but, much more seriously, for so-called political motives. That happened in Russia, Czechoslovakia and Yugoslavia.

Young Clara Becker could never remember any other home than the luxurious apartment which her parents owned in St. Petersburg (now Leningrad). She knew she had been adopted when the childless Beckers were already middle-aged, but she never troubled her head about her origins. All she knew was that she was Russian-born and that her adoptive parents were Estonian. The Beckers lived in the old part of the city near to the Imperial Palace and mixed only with the aristocracy.

That meant a lonely childhood for Clara. She rarely met other children, for the families of her parents' friends were already grown up. She was never allowed to go out alone but must be accompanied by a governess or a servant. So this intelligent, grave-faced girl watched the street life and the boats that sailed on the smooth waters of the Neva from the windows of the spacious apartment. The only excitement in the home seemed to be when the polishers made their monthly visit. The inlaid parquet floors needed the regular attention of these experts and Clara delighted in seeing them polish the long corridors and grand salon, brushes strapped to their feet as though they were skates. She longed to try it herself but her weight would not have been sufficient to produce the right satiny sheen on the wood.

The dressmaker was another welcome visitor. She stayed for two months each time, making new clothes for the family. At least she was someone to talk to, and while her hands were busy she could answer the many questions the girl asked. She encouraged Clara to bring her books and show her pictures. One was a finely illustrated life of Christ, though Clara knew little of the meaning of the coloured plates. The dressmaker was a Christian and she took time to explain the gospel story to the wide-eyed girl.

The Becker family always spoke German together but Russian with the servants, so Clara was bi-lingual. Then she was given a French governess and was soon chattering to her dolls in French, though quite frankly she preferred books to dolls. The next governess was English, so that by the time she was eleven the girl was fluent in four languages. A great event lay on the horizon. She was to start school, a special preparatory establishment for the daughters of the rich, to carry them from the governess stage to university. Clara was excited but also nervous, not on account of the lessons, for she had a quick mind, but because she would have to mix with other girls, which she dreaded.

Her form-mistress was a practising Christian. When she found that Clara was interested in religious matters, she advised her to go to Sunday school. Clara was dubious about her parents' reactions, but it was worth trying. To her delight they agreed, making the proviso that she must be accompanied there and back by a maid, as was done for day school.

To obtain a Bible of her own Clara had to resort to further strategy. She saved up her pocket-money, and then mentioned casually to her mother one day that her teacher would like her to have a Bible for study. A beautifully bound volume was bought. Clara found it dull! Her teacher, quick to seize the opportunity, gave the girl a St. John's Gospel in English. This provided Bible knowledge *and* language study. Clara was delighted. She read it over so many times that she soon knew it by heart.

When Clara was seventeen she attended a meeting led by a woman evangelist, a select gathering for the daughters of aristocrats only. That afternoon God revealed Himself through the speaker to the seeking girl. After the meeting Clara asked for spiritual guidance and was told, 'When you find a text that you feel is for you, put your name in it.' In her evening prayer period, Clara took that advice with a favourite text, saying aloud with all earnestness, 'If with all her heart Clara Becker truly seeks Me, she shall surely find Me.' At last she felt that she had found Christ as her Saviour and friend.

As a student, Clara attended her first Salvation Army meeting in St. Petersburg on Ascension Day, 1915. It was held in a large flat, the folding doors open from room to room to accommodate those who came to listen. There was a mixed audience of aristocrats, students and peasants.

Studies took most of Clara's time until she passed her final examinations as a teacher; then again she attended an Army meeting and, in response to an appeal, walked forward to kneel at the plain kitchen chair which served as a Penitent Form. At that moment she placed her whole life at God's disposal.

She was twenty-five years old when she trained as a Salvation Army officer in 1917. There was then no training college in Russia and conditions of living were becoming very chaotic, with shortage of food and household articles, because the dark clouds of changing political climate loomed ahead. Clara was sent to Helsinki, Finland, for her training, thereby adding two other languages, Finnish and Swedish, to her linguistic repertoire. She was then appointed to help with secretarial duties back in St. Petersburg.

The food situation had become desperate. Hardly anyone had bread to eat except the sour black bread which needed so much chewing. At any rate it gave a feeling of fullness in the stomach, although dried lichen had been mixed with the flour to eke it out. Real griping hunger-pangs were known by children and adults alike. Cabbage soup was not filling either, especially when most of it was water. Horse-meat was a luxury few could afford.

The famine brought sickness and death in its train, for undernourished bodies had no resistance to disease. Smallpox claimed many victims. One day Clara got a message that a Swedish girl-captain from the Children's Home was in hospital. She hurried to visit her but arrived too late. Clara recalls the painful moments:

> We went to the mortuary to identify the Captain's body and found the place filled with naked corpses covered with dirty sheets. It was impossible to move among them without touching the bodies, and the air became black as a swarm of flies buzzed up. We recognised our comrade by her fair hair; for the rest, the disease had so disfigured her face as to make her unrecognisable.

Coffins were exorbitantly dear but Clara's parents paid for one so that the beloved officer could be laid to rest decently and not just thrown naked into a communal grave.

For some years Clara served in secretarial work and children's work, but the revolution in Russia created serious difficulties for the little band of salvationists. She took a government position during the day to ensure a salary and spent her evenings at the Children's Home. To feed the five children for whom the officers had taken responsibility became a great problem.

One day as Clara was approaching the flat she was warned by a neighbour that her comrade officer had been arrested and that the children were under armed guard. The captain's wife had entered hospital a few hours earlier for the birth of her first child. She was exhausted and undernourished and as no food was supplied by the hospital for the patients (there being none available), the captain had been out in search of food for his wife and arrested on his return. From the friendly neighbour Clara begged a little food to take to the new mother in hospital, though she dared not tell her of her husband's arrest.

Imperative in Clara's mind was the need to get news through

to Army leaders in London and Helsinki, telling of the dangerous developments. Strict censorship of letters was imposed, but she found a solution. Writing in English she simply stated that 'a number of our families are with Paul and Silas in Acts 16'. She knew it would convey the fact that they were in prison. Then Clara faced a costly decision. She must return to the flat herself, even though it meant certain arrest.

She was admitted by an armed guard and taken to police headquarters next day for a five-hour interrogation. Then she was pushed into a tiny cell barely high enough to stand up in. With a wry smile she blessed her own short stature. Later in the day she was again searched. Even her dark thick plaited hair was unwound in case she had hidden something forbidden there. Most of her few possessions were taken from her, including her New Testament.

Solitary confinement is a harsh test and Clara prayed much of the time. One day she heard a gruff voice call her name: 'Becker!' With thumping heart she followed the guard out into the dingy corridor where she met nine men — all of them named Becker! So the ten Beckers were driven off in a lorry to another prison and Clara was placed in another narrow cell.

On the third night the key in the door was turned and a woman was pushed in. In a flash the two recognised each other but restrained their joy. Two salvationists in one small cell! The prisoners got very little food and were kept alive by what their friends could bring them — a little cold porridge or a potato baked in its skin in the ashes of a fire.

Weeks passed and Easter Sunday morning came. The guard came too. He spoke but three words to Clara Becker: 'You are free.'

A few days later she sat in the train on the way to relatives in Estonia. From there she continued to London where she took up service in the Army's translations bureau until her retirement.

* * *

The Salvation Army has also operated in Yugoslavia, the homeland of Mary Lichtenberger. Mary, daughter of a British and Foreign Bible Society colporteur, received her training for officership in London but was then sent to Czechoslovakia, there being as yet no Army work in her own land. With German she was proficient and one in three among the Czechs spoke that language. Her good-natured and spirited approach to her duties made her popular among the converts and soldiers. She was dismayed, though, when she was asked to interpret their dreams!

It happened after a sermon she had preached about Joseph having been given by God the interpretation of Pharaoh's dream. One of the men came to her to recount a vivid dream he had had and to implore her to interpret it for him. This she laughingly refused to attempt, but the story got round that Captain Lichtenberger could interpret dreams but was reluctant to use her talent. One day when Mary went to the pubs to sell her *War Cry* the barman called out, 'Here comes the fortune-teller.' There was loud laughter as a man planted himself before the salvationist, his hand outstretched. 'Can you read the future from my palm?' he asked mockingly. 'Yes, I can,' was the cool reply. She took his hand, studied it for a moment and then quoted, 'It is appointed unto man once to die and after death the judgment.' The unexpected answer brought instant silence.

In 1934 came the day that Mary had long prayed for. Army work was to begin in Yugoslavia, her homeland. An officer-couple had been sent as pioneers. The General had given magnanimous assistance in the form of £50 in cash, an Army flag, and the services of Captain Mary Lichtenberger.

The first problem was to find a hall in Belgrade that they could use. Street after street they searched, their little cash ready for a down-payment. The most it would stretch to was the rent of an empty and dirty public-house. By knocking down walls between the bars, they achieved accommodation for two hundred persons. It was good that the three officers had learnt not only theology but 'scrubology' in the training college, for soon their knees were red and sore as they scoured away at the beer-stained wooden floors. Whitewash on the walls gave a clean background for the texts in Cyrillic letters which a sign-writer painted for them.

The first meeting achieved full house, with folk packed into doorways and passages. Many nationalities were present. The Army leader spoke in German, with Mary translating sentence by sentence into Serbian. One of the earliest converts was a young Slovak, freed after two years in prison. His crime was a serious one. As a lad of fourteen he had killed his father with an axe to defend his mother from ill-treatment. He was glad to find friends in the Army.

When the pioneering period was successfully weathered, the married leaders were sent to another country, leaving Mary Lichtenberger in sole charge. Her first thought was to start a *War Cry* in Serbian but she had to be journalist, editor and seller of the new paper. For each issue she translated four Army songs which the people could then sing in the meetings. The joyful singing of the British salvationists was still, for Mary, a cherished memory, a strong contrast to the Orthodox Church chanting in Yugoslavia. She found it a difficult task to fit the long Serbian words into the short English musical phrases, but once the congregation knew the tunes they seemed to like to join in heartily. By translating and using four new songs each month in the *War Cry*, the energetic captain was finally able to publish an Army song book in Serbian, with two hundred songs. Her heart glowed with a sense of satisfaction as she heard her people sing them. She knew that the words of a song would often remain in the memory longer than the spoken message.

Then, while walking round the streets, Captain Mary noticed many poor children who looked half-starved, so her next enterprise was to start the free distribution of hot soup to one hundred children each midday. One girl gained fifteen pounds in weight in three months.

One day to her great surprise Mary found a letter with the royal coat of arms among her mail. Queen Mary of Yugoslavia wished to receive her in audience next morning. Queen Mary was the great-grand-daughter of Queen Victoria. She was interested in the Christmas relief which the Army was distributing to the poor, to which she always contributed two dozen food parcels. Captain Mary was able to tell her also about the soup distribution to children. A half-hour elapsed before the Queen stood up, a sign for Mary and her companion to leave.

All this time she was conducting meetings and had gradually won a group of converts and friends round her. By 1941 a second corps had been opened, and an outpost. There were youth groups, women's fellowships, a small brass band and a guitar band. When one of her soldiers died, Mary claimed the right to officiate at the funeral in Army tradition. Even greater interest was aroused when she conducted the first salvationist wedding.

The Second World War caused a political upheaval and daily living became hazardous. In 1944 under the communist regime the meeting-hall was confiscated and turned into a dancing saloon. The salvationists moved into the basement where previously the soup kitchen had functioned. In one gathering every member present was hit by stones thrown through the broken windows. Finally the downstairs hall was seized and the group met in a tiny room. All Army property had been confiscated by the government, so there were only trunks and suitcases to sit on for those who still came to worship.

Two final blows fell. All Army comrades were summoned and forced to sign a promise that they would never again meet together with Mary Lichtenberger. Children were forbidden to attend her Sunday school. In September 1948 Mary was arrested. She was offered her freedom if she would agree to spy on people and report to the authorities, but that she refused to do. She determined to use her imprisonment to continue her efforts to evangelise. Fortunately she had been allowed to keep her Bible and when opportunity was given, she would sit down with a fellow-prisoner and read and explain the Scriptures. The prison officials watched Mary closely. She was an unusual type of customer for them. One of the more friendly ones said to her one day, 'You know, we admire you. You are the bravest woman in this prison.'

Years passed. No one knew what had become of Mary Lichtenberger. One day a poorly-dressed woman, thin and ill, came to the Salvation Army headquarters in London and asked to see the General. It was Mary, formerly the leader of Army activities in Yugoslavia, now a homeless refugee. When her story was told, arrangements were made for her to transfer to Canada to complete her service and retire.

*   *   *

Major Marie Ozanne was a saint; that was the consensus of opinion about her by all who knew her intimately. She was a

Channel Islander from Guernsey, so her knowledge of French made her useful for Army service on the Continent and, after some years in France she was transferred to Belgium. She was busy at her task there when Belgium was invaded during the Second World War, and Marie had to return to Guernsey. There she reported for Salvation Army duty and was given the responsibility of St. Sampson's corps.

Then it was the turn of the Channel Isles to be invaded. Salvationist activities were forbidden. Marie Ozanne was made of inner granite and she simply — in her saintly innocence — continued her pastoral duties in full uniform. Every Saturday afternoon she stood in the market-place reading her Bible and talking to those who dared stop to listen. That was too much for the invading authorities and they confiscated her uniform. Marie was undeterred. God's work called to be done and she had consecrated her life to do it. She continued her ministry in civilian clothes. Not only did she visit and pray with the islanders but also she tackled the study of German. The invaders needed God too.

In the homes she visited she gathered small groups for prayer. Once a week she met the womenfolk, all of them harassed by shortage of food, and by anxiety for their menfolk and for their children's future. To them she spoke hopefully of faith in God and His love, strengthening their morale and imbuing them with fresh courage.

Most of the school-children had been evacuated, but now the smallest ones were reaching school age. Marie, who had been a primary teacher before officership, was asked to teach them. She weighed the matter carefully, then decided not to accept the offer. It would certainly have meant an easier life for her, but she felt that all her time and energies must be consecrated to her spiritual task.

Then some unknown person painted a large letter V on public monuments and it was announced that unless the guilty one confessed all the islanders would be punished. Marie Ozanne wrote to the occupation authorities and offered to die in the nameless one's place to save her compatriots from vengeance. Her offer was not accepted. When some Frenchmen were charged with an act of sabotage of which they were innocent, she volunteered to be shot in their place. This also was refused.

The internee camp was quite close to where Marie lived and she was horrified to hear constant screams from those undergoing floggings and, possibly, torture. She was already known to the occupation forces, for she had vigorously protested more than once on behalf of the islanders who had to endure forced labour of a particularly rigorous kind.

Marie Ozanne never shirked what she felt to be her duty as a Christian, however much it might cost her. She asked to speak to the camp commandant. This thin, undernourished woman faced him with serene courage and made a strong protest against the ill-treatment meted out to prisoners. Such a troublesome saint was anathema to officialdom and at last Marie was sent to prison. From her cell she wrote messages of Christian witness and encouragement; within the prison her calm and radiant spirit cheered those suffering with her.

Liberation came because her health was failing rapidly. In her final weeks she still sent notes of spiritual encouragement and prayed with those who visited her. She was only thirty-eight years old when she died in February 1943.

CHAPTER SIX

'My Best Men are Women'

'MY best men are women.' William Booth himself is credited with this statement. He had good reason to make it. Women were showing themselves capable of leadership, even of pioneering against a climate of fierce opposition. Assailed by mockery as well as by missiles they pursued an undeviating course. In several lands women held long-term high command, building up an Army structure that has stood the tests of a near-century.

Evangeline Booth, William's daughter, holds the record of the longest female leadership in the Army's history, that of Commander in the United States for thirty years, followed by Generalship of the whole Army from 1934 to 1939. She was a born leader with natural gifts of oratory, a sparkling wit at its best in rapid repartee, and sublime courage in face of both physical and moral opposition.

When she was only ten her father heard her preach on the subject 'God is love' with such power and earnestness that he made notes of what she said, remarking, 'Eva is the orator of the family.' It does not detract from her eloquence to learn that the sermon was delivered to an audience of dolls, brooms and cushions in the confines of the playroom at home.

Converted at twelve years of age, she ran home with flashing eyes and glowing cheeks to tell the good news. From then on she was launched into the salvation war. In her teens she visited pubs to sing and speak of God's love. Dressed like a flower-girl, in crumpled clothes, she spent a day among them to get to know their living conditions. As captain of a London corps with a large meeting-hall, she managed to fill it night after night with people eager to hear her impassioned appeals for decisions for Christ. John Bright, the Quaker statesman, used to slip into a back seat of the great hall in Marylebone to listen to her.

The exploits of this teenage captain attracted the attention of a number of public-spirited men. Lord Onslow, Earl Cairns and the Earl of Shaftesbury expressed a desire to meet her. She received word to report at the Houses of Parliament.

'Come, my child,' said Lord Chancellor Cairns, 'just talk to us as if we were listening to you on the pavement.'

'Look on me as a drunkard,' said the Earl of Shaftesbury. 'What exactly would you say to me?'

'I should say that you are a fine fellow,' replied Eva, 'and I should want to know why you treated yourself like that, spoiling your looks and making yourself ridiculous. I should say to you that you are worth more than that, and it is time you should know it.'

'But if I replied that I couldn't help it?'

'I should ask you to kneel with me,' said the young captain, 'and ask for God's help.'

'If I was not quite convinced?'

'I should remind you of Christ on the Cross. He died to save and He did not die for nothing.'

'That is what you mean by the gospel?' asked Earl Cairns gravely.

'Yes, sir, that is what we mean by the gospel.'

At twenty-three years of age Eva Booth was placed in charge of all the Army's evangelical centres in London in addition to having the oversight of the training-homes. It was a time of turbulence and persecution for salvationists, and Eva received her share of brickbats and abuse, but her quick-wittedness and astounding audacity got her out of many tight corners. In one open-air gathering a man threw a sharp stone which cut Eva's arm. Undaunted she marched up to him demanding, 'Bandage this, quick! You did it, you fix it!' The man not only put a temporary bandage on her arm but also later joined the Army.

Meanwhile, at a time of riots in Torquay, Eva was sent down to encourage salvationists who were being harassed by ruffians.

To put an end to such religious persecution the Fowler Bill was being introduced in the House of Commons and it was there that the battle against unjust opposition was finally won. Eva was called back to London to give evidence before a select committee. Legal advisers told her to answer all questions with a simple Yes or No but events took an unexpected turn. Sir Charles Russell, appointed Chairman of the committee, was a famous criminal lawyer, feared for his persistent cross-questioning. He looked at the Army's chief witness, this bright-faced girl in her bonnet; then in a quiet and friendly voice said, 'Now, my child, come up here and sit with me and tell me all about it.' The crowded room was silent as the two conversed, and the Bill was passed.

In 1896, at thirty-one years of age, Commander Eva was appointed as leader of the quickly growing Army in Canada. She had a strongly developed dramatic sense; loving vivid colours and martial music, she was enthralled by pageantry and giant processions. Fond of riding also, she rode daily to her headquarters in Toronto with a red cape flying from her shoulders and a red hat perched on her head.

New York welcomed her as leader in 1904 and throughout the thirty years she remained in charge she continued to be colourful, dynamic and passionate in God's service. In addition to her administrative gifts and oratory, she poured her soul into songs which gripped the heart and conscience and which carried her name around the international Army. But the early days in America were not easy. At one gathering she was hissed and could not make herself heard. Hurriedly leaving the platform she returned with the Stars and Stripes wrapped round her. 'Hiss if you dare,' she challenged. Dead silence! She went on to win the crowd with her eloquence.

Eva had a tremendous capacity for work. Her early morning health programme, usually a ride or a swim, maintained her vigour, and a jealously guarded time for private prayer kept her heart in tune with God.

It was to a heavy and onerous position that Evangeline Booth was elected in 1934 as the first woman General of The Salvation Army, a position she held until her retirement in 1939 at the age of seventy-four. In her speech of acceptance after the polling her humour gleamed. 'This general arrangement is the nearest to the marriage altar that I have ever come. You have taken me "for better or for worse".'

When asked what had been her finest experience, the General recounted a day spent at the Puthencruz Leper Colony in Southern India. A choir of small girls had trained zealously to sing one of Evangeline Booth's own compositions, 'The World for God'. With emotion she recalled, 'Their hands and faces were badly scarred but their voices were clear and true. When they came to the words in the song, "with all my heart, I'll do my part" they put their tiny marred hands over their hearts. I was overcome. Their faith and their light was so much greater than mine. I felt humble, seeing them.'

Towards the end of her life General Eva admitted that she had only one regret and that was that she had only one life to live. 'I have worked hard. I've made every sacrifice that has been asked of me with a smile in my heart as well as on my face. I would not change one day or take back one hour. You don't get real joy from jewels. The joy from social attainments is nice but it soon passes. The joy of service to the poor and unfortunate is lasting and blessed.'

*   *   *

It was not only young, enthusiastic teenagers who were called to pioneer Army work. In Sweden it was a mature woman, Hanna Ouchterlony, already forty-four years of age. She was an educated woman who had opened a religious bookshop in the ground floor of her house. Some Scotch blood from her forefathers ran in her veins. Drawn to religion by inherent interest, she had already made progress in her Christian experience but she yearned for more.

God, who 'works in a mysterious way His wonders to perform', was to use the convalescence of young Bramwell Booth to push Miss Ouchterlony into the top leadership of a movement of which she had no previous knowledge. Bramwell, William Booth's twenty-two-year-old son, was resting in the home of some friends of the family in Värnamo, Sweden, where he held house meetings. Hanna attended and the deep experience he revealed of the things of God captivated her. Here was the kind of religion her heart had been hungering for. She accepted with joy an invitation to spend a few months in the Founder's home in Clapton, London, and returned to her homeland wearing an Army brooch.

On a later visit to England she was given the rank of major, returning to Sweden in 1882 to start Army operations with the assistance of a handful of helpers. On the Feast of the Innocents five salvationists marched with the newly-dedicated flag to a large theatre in Stockholm. The invading troop was composed of Major Hanna, Lieutenants Jenny and Emily, and two men officers. Major Hanna preached, Jenny of the sweet face and clear voice sang and played her guitar, Emily testified, and the two young men alternately beat the drum, spoke or kept order.

Right from the beginning the meetings were crowded and disturbances were caused by those outside fighting to gain admittance. The police imposed fines and even imprisonments to limit the length of the gatherings. At one time the uniform was reported to be objectionable, so Hanna Ouchterlony had to stand before the magistrate and be examined with a critical eye. He found no fault with it. Later the police imposed a fine on Major Hanna, but she refused to pay it and dared them to send her to prison. They never did.

After only eight days Major Hanna had fifty recruits. They were no longer 'innocents'. They were being trained in heavenly warfare with earthly tactics, for opposition against them increased. Fireworks were thrown at them. Lives were threatened. The police gave orders that the officers must ride in a sledge from the meetings, escorted by a police sledge. What a delightful Stockholm idyll, with the cold moon reflected in a myriad sparkles from the frost and snow crystals! In Gothenburg rats were let loose in the hall, but the women 'warriors for Jesus' kept the initiative and soon it was triumphantly reported that 'the devil flees, chased by salvationist coastguardsmen'.

Rowdyism by hooligans in the meetings in Stockholm reached such an alarming stage that the police forbade any more gatherings in the halls. This was a stiff sentence in the winter cold, but salvationists responded by arranging back-yard

meetings with a cart as a platform and empty packing cases as
seats for those who preferred not to stand in the deep snow.
Converts were made. Membership increased to hundreds, thousands. Major Hanna even organised sea manoeuvres to take the
gospel to towns along the lakes and coasts, and out in the pine
forests great spiritual battles were fought out to a triumphant
finish.

They were glorious days, filled with the thrill of pioneering,
of building and expanding. Soon the work became more established and settled into the steady rhythm of goodwill and social
work, day nurseries, large well-functioning corps, and youth
activities of every kind.

One day a little girl came to the Stockholm 3 corps and
begged earnestly to be given a part in the Christmas play which
the Sunday-school children were preparing. She was made welcome and given a small role. Her name was Greta Gustafsson,
later to be known as Greta Garbo. The producer of the children's play remarked afterwards that Greta seemed to have a
decided talent for acting.

For ten years Hanna Ouchterlony continued as the leader of
Salvation Army operations in Sweden. To commemorate her
intrepid pioneering a bronze bust has been unveiled in her
honour in the central park of her home-town Värnamo. Hanna
is shown wearing her Army bonnet, ribbons tied under the chin,
her uniform primly buttoned high at the neck. It is a permanent
reminder of one who responded to the call of God.

Commissioner Ouchterlony, as she became, later pioneered
the Army's opening in Norway and remained there as leader for
six years. Norway received the salvationists with more good will
than Sweden had done.

The fisher-folk in the far north were not forgotten. Theirs
was a hard life, facing stormy seas, long dark winters, sleet and

snow. A Salvation Army lifeboat named the *Catherine Booth* and manned by salvationists was launched in February 1900. Ouchterlony's injunction to the crew was typical: 'Don't forget the people's souls when you rescue their bodies.'

*   *   *

Finland is another of the European lands where a woman held the reins of leadership during the stormy first years while The Salvation Army was establishing itself in the affections of the people. Hedvig von Haartman was appointed as leader of the young movement a few months after its inception and remained as the Army's head from 1890 to 1898.

Hedvig had had an exceptionally happy childhood, learning to ride and drive, sail and fish, skate and ski. After university studies she was sent to Switzerland and Paris for two years to complete her knowledge of French before taking up a position as teacher of that language. In her home she had learnt Christian truths and principles, but within her there smouldered a longing after a more profound experience. One night after a revival service she gave herself fully to God. Wondering how she could best use her life to bring others to Christ, she decided to become a nurse. She was brusquely told that a hospital was no place for a fanatic!

Later she met The Salvation Army through a friend's recommendation and felt that her place must be there. Months of training in London gave her experience of handling roughs and visiting slum homes, something far removed from her former sheltered life. When she returned to Finland with Lieutenant's rank her friends commented, 'She is the same and yet different. The power of God is upon her.'

Her headquarters were a workman's cottage in a side street. By day Hedvig visited the people in their homes and at night she spoke in the meetings. The pioneers lived in real poverty with only the simplest food to eat. One day Hedvig found a hole in the sole of her boots and had no money to get them mended. In Helsinki she had scores of wealthy relatives and friends but to them she would not turn. Instead she prayed about it, and there in the mud she saw a silver coin which someone had dropped.

Into her headquarters-cottage she received her first three cadets to train them for officership. It was a tight squeeze. Her own bed had to be pushed behind a screen in the dining-room. The new trainees had rather vague ideas about 'helping dear Miss von Haartman', but she put them through a rigorous discipline of duties and studies, blowing a whistle to wake them in the morning in true 'training-home' style. She herself had to tackle the production of a *War Cry* without any previous knowledge of journalism or press work. She groaned inwardly as she sent out her first issue, prepared with infinite effort yet, she well knew, of no high standard. She learnt by experience — the school of all pioneers — improving on her own mistakes.

Corps were opened throughout Finland, some Swedish-speaking, some Finnish, when an event occurred which might have had serious consequences. The Army's progress attracted the attention of the Russian government under whose jurisdiction Finland then stood. Would an international organisation such as The Salvation Army be allowed to continue? Hedvig von Haartman prepared for the crisis with military precision. She was summoned to the Governor. In advance she sent him a copy of William Booth's *In Darkest England and the Way Out*. She called her soldiers to prayer and herself spent the greater part of the preceding night on her knees, pleading with God for His help. Next morning, in her neat uniform, she met the Governor, who was greatly impressed by her calm dignity and the way she presented the Army's case. To her great joy he gave his consent for the continuation of the work with slight modifications.

The history of The Salvation Army in Finland is very like that of Sweden. Meetings were disturbed by ruffians. There were police charges, imprisonments, financial difficulties, bundles of the *War Cry* seized ... yet once again God brought His soldiers through triumphantly. It came as a great blow when in 1898 the beloved Hedvig von Haartman was transferred to German Switzerland as leader. It meant learning another language, her fifth, but she tackled it with dauntless courage. God had something wonderful in reserve for her in Switzerland. There she met a man officer, a former professor of botany at Zurich university, and they were married under the Army flag.

It would be good if one could leave the story there, with a happy ending ringing joybells in the mind, but the physical weakness from which Hedvig had suffered for years began to take its toll. The honeymoon was to be taken in Finland, her own homeland, but it was two years before they could make the journey. Once more she stood upon the Temple platform in Helsinki to preach to those who knew and loved her, but the price of her involvement was collapse. She died in Hamburg on the way back to Switzerland, only forty-two years old.

*   *   *

The stories told in this chapter demonstrate that William Booth was right when he gave women positions of authority and influence. His shrewd judgment was justified. Unfortunately the line of women leaders has thinned successively since his days.

This can best be seen in focus in the High Council, the collective body of top Army leaders from the whole world, which meets only to choose a new General. In 1963 there were forty-nine High Councillors of which three were women. In 1969, the last High Council, there were forty-five delegates, of which two were women.

Laura Petri, Phil.Dr., of Sweden, a former slum officer, gave a radio lecture in 1948 on the subject of 'The Woman Officer of The Salvation Army'. She commented, 'It is more difficult for women to reach the higher positions than for men. To be advanced a man requires hardly more than average gifts. A woman must be superior.'

However, some women have achieved top or near-top leadership in the last two decades, as shown in the following two stories.

Anyone who met Commissioner Emma Davies agreed that she was a tonic, a buoyant, colourful personality radiating good cheer and good sense. Warm in speech and manner, she was every inch a leader. Resourceful and courageous, she tackled any situation which arose in her forthright, capable manner.

Leaders recognised Emma Davies's potential very early, and soon after her commissioning as an officer in 1917 she was shuttle-cocked backwards and forwards across the world to gain a variety of experience. Appointments in Great Britain, Canada and New Zealand were a prelude to her taking command of a field division in England. Training-college work followed, and then a surprise appointment as the Army's leader in Ceylon in 1947.

Emma Davies was one of those people whom men and women alike respect, and it was never any real problem for her to have men officers under her command. She *was* the leader. In

Colombo she took turns with the bishops and other religious leaders to broadcast to millions of unseen listeners in the East, as far away as Hong Kong and Singapore. Her signature tune, 'It is summertime in my heart', will long be remembered. It was sung, whistled and hummed by thousands of her regular fans long after she had left the shores of Ceylon. She was an excellent speaker with a wealth of vivid illustration which stuck in the mind and nailed her message home.

This leader had her domesticated side which she called her 'Friday secret'. Each Friday afternoon the housewife took over, and Emma enjoyed a frenzy of housework, gardening or cooking, and while the jobs were tackled, one by one, problems would be sorted out in her mind until she could see the right solution. It was a kind of work therapy. Her weekends were spent in public engagements, for she never spared herself. It was a heavy, taxing programme, but Emma Davies met all the demands.

After Ceylon came the leadership of the Madras and Telegu territory, and finally of the Women's Social Services in Great Britain and Ireland. Shortly before her retirement in 1960 Commissioner Davies was asked to conduct campaigns in the East, Australasia, Canada and the United States, and so her active service finished with a whirl of international engagements.

Looking back over her life Emma Davies confessed, 'When young I was intolerant. As I have learned of the sufferings and heroism of others, I have been helped towards a sympathetic nature. I have learnt that non-essentials are not worth fighting over. What really matters is constantly enjoying the smile and approval of God.'

Then came the peace of a quiet cottage, tending the roses and enjoying her friends. But not for long! God called her out again and again for a triumphant sortie. The end came unexpectedly in 1970, but Emma was ready.

*   *   *

Cheerful, outgoing Gladys Calliss was always very popular as a youth leader in Australia. Young folk liked her contagious good spirits and her daring leadership on evangelisation jaunts to out-lying places. She had learnt to be resourceful as a salvationist in Colonel Light Gardens corps, Adelaide, before the corps moved into its new and imposing edifice, and in the older, rougher days before she entered the Army's training college in Melbourne in 1935.

She had already been an officer for ten years when she felt a direct call from God to serve Him in Indonesia. It was with some trepidation that she informed her leaders of her feelings. Her application was sympathetically considered, but it was not until 1947 that she landed in Kalawara, mid-Celebes, which was to be her working area for many adventurous years.

The Army's work in central Celebes lies in mountainous districts where the narrow, stony paths cross deep ravines, and raging torrents have to be traversed by fragile-looking bridges of twisted cane ropes. The small villages are tucked away in almost inaccessible places, the houses perched high on poles driven into the ground. Sometimes it is possible to reach the villages by bullock cart or on horseback, but more often one must climb step by step over stony trails, with a deep drop at one side and steeply rising cliffs on the other. The densely growing jungle, beautiful but frightening, hides many a wild beast hungry enough to attack. Snakes of many colours abound in the undergrowth and overhead magnificent butterflies, some with the wing-span of a bird, gleaming red, orange, blue and green, flit among the orchids.

Into this green luxuriance came Captain Gladys Calliss straight from sun-baked Australia. She soon learnt to cling to her horse as it stumbled down an almost impossibly steep mountain track, or to wade knee-deep in mud after heavy rainfall and to trust her rather heavily-built frame to the swaying rattan bridges strung over rushing rivers. She found it eerie to follow a narrow jungle path with the overhead foliage so dense that no sunlight could trickle through it. In the dim light, following the muddy, slippery path, one had to look out for snakes, monkeys, wild pigs and deer, and from time to time halt to pick leeches from legs or arms. It was not long before Gladys learned to carry with her a bamboo shaft filled with soapy water to deal with that pest. Leeches have an aversion to soap!

The people of Celebes were earlier notorious as head-hunters. Human heads or scalps were buried under heathen temples or even under homes by witch doctors to the accompaniment of dancing and incantations, to propitiate the evil spirits of earth. It was through ignorance that these superstitions were followed. Once the Christian message was heard, there was an encouraging response and pioneer salvationists had already established both corps and schools.

The Toradja people, as they are called, make good Christians once they have taken their stand. They have proved themselves willing to suffer for their faith and they themselves go out as messengers to their own folk, sitting on the earthen floors of the small wooden huts to teach the Christian faith. As salvationists they are loyal and hardworking, using their free time to cut down trees in the jungle in order to build halls and schools.

Gladys had to learn two new languages, Dutch and Indonesian, and to adapt to primitive living. Firewood had to be picked up in the bush, lighting was by kerosene lamps only, and water drawn from a well had to be boiled for ten minutes before it was drinkable. Bread was baked in kerosene tins. It was inevitable that there were moments of homesickness, especially when on clear nights the Southern Cross loomed so near.

But she was soon engaged in visiting the district, sometimes having to be away for ten days or a fortnight at a time. Contact could be made with the people on the long and tiring journeys, for there were always some out in the jungle searching for resin to sell or gathering stems of climbing plants to twist into cane rope. Some might be working in the small gardens they cleared on the mountain slopes, where a few vegetables could be grown.

On arrival at a village with an Army corps and school, Gladys and her companions would be met by the boys' flute band and singing salvationists waving the Army flag. Events crowded the programme from daylight into the night hours. There would be new recruits and soldiers to be enrolled. How moving it was for her to see one-time leaders of devil-worship giving their pledges to God under the flag! Then there were always babies to be dedicated, sometimes as many as thirty in one place. Gladys loved taking the fat brown youngsters in her arms and blessing them in God's name. If any baby whimpered during the ceremony, its mother simply lifted her blouse and fed it from her ample breast. Occasionally there would be a wedding to perform and sometimes a funeral. One had to be prepared for anything.

In time the captain got used to the interest her appearance aroused. It was not uncommon for a crowd to gather round her, making remarks quite openly. Some of the old grannies would even come and poke her arms and legs (which admittedly were rather large) and would make complimentary remarks about her double chin! As long as they accepted her Gladys did not mind.

The Toradja men usually wear shirt and shorts but the women keep to the traditional dress of a three-tiered bark-cloth skirt with a bark-cloth blouse. On Sundays, however, the women pretty themselves by using yards and yards of brightly coloured material, obtaining the three-tiered effect by ingeniously winding it round their bodies. Captain Gladys always saved up her few coloured magazines to show the people. One day there was a photograph of Queen Elizabeth at a garden party wearing a three-tiered skirt of silk. How excited the Toradja women became. They danced with glee chanting, 'The Great Queen of England wears a Toradja dress like we do!'

These journeys were not without adventure. Once a jeep loaded with resin had been lent to the party to take them down the mountain track. Unfortunately there was a blow-out, but the jeep tipped into the gutter and not over the precipice as it might have done. Jumping out, they had to unload their own luggage and nine hundred kilos of resin belonging to the jeep's owner! After getting the vehicle on to the road, they loaded up again and continued, only to find that a river they had to cross was in flood. Moments of consultation gave birth to an idea. Everyone collected large stones and hurled them into the river-bed with the idea of making a shallow-enough crossing for the jeep. For over an hour they lifted and threw rocks and stones. Then a cautious crossing was essayed, and succeeded until the trailer hit the opposite bank and refused to budge any further. There was nothing for it but to unload all the baggage again, including the sacks of resin, climb the bank with them and re-pack. In all, it took the party four hours to do the twenty-five-mile journey.

On another day, real danger was added to the spice of life.

While the swaying bullock cart slowly negotiated the river crossing, a loud roaring was heard in the distance. The boys recognised it as the sound of flood waters coming. They whipped the bullocks madly, urging them on, while Gladys clung to the sides of the lunging cart, and prayed. After a few terrifying minutes they reached the opposite bank just ahead of a wall of water carrying trees and huge boulders which swept over the place they had crossed, and crashed further down into the valley.

Normally quite robust, Gladys suffered a few unpleasant attacks of illness caused by the rough travelling and living conditions when on trek. She wrote to a friend, 'Muscular rheumatism in my head and neck is hardly a comfortable complaint when one is touring in a springless bullock cart. For the first time for five weeks I can turn my head a bit, but there is one lovely blessing with this illness — my clothes are now too big and I'm so happy about that.'

After two years of intensive campaigning Gladys felt completely exhausted. Her time of annual holiday drew near and she made a choice of place that was unusual. She would go to a high mountain village and live alone with her house-girl for the three weeks. Colleagues said she would be bored long before the time expired but they were wrong. Gladys revelled in the silence (the thin walls of her room in Kalawara let in all sounds day and night), the leisure, the chance to read, think and pray, and to sing aloud those songs in her own language that had meant most for her spiritual development. It was so long since she had heard any English. She was the only Britisher in mid-Celebes.

Salvationists in the little village prepared to give their leader the solitude she desired. They lent her a tiny two-roomed bamboo hut. True, the wind penetrated both walls and floors but Gladys told herself that ventilation was necessary and desirable. The kind friends even made her a 'bathroom' by inserting a bamboo into a mountain stream so that the icy water cascaded in a shower. Six huge bamboos made a sturdy platform on which she could stand while she bathed, and a screen of palm leaves shielded her from the gaze of onlookers. The screen came only as high as her chin, but you have to be grateful for small mercies, she grinned to herself. Three weeks of that retreat and the captain came back to her task refreshed in body, soul and spirit.

Back at work she wrote to a friend:

There is an outbreak of tropical ulcers, especially among the school-children, and several times a day I have to drop my work to cleanse and bandage the limbs of several of them. How glad I am that I took first-aid lessons in Australia. God helps me wonderfully to do things that I would naturally shrink from. It is wonderful to see an ulcer two inches square and deep begin to heal up and healthy skin start to grow. I am a very happy and privileged person.

Under Gladys's vigorous leadership the work expanded. Meeting-halls and school buildings were erected in a number of villages, the Toradja salvationists carrying hundreds of sheets of corrugated iron on their backs for over twenty-five miles up mountain paths in order to roof their new properties. Others gathered stones and sand from the river-beds and helped in teams to drag huge logs from the forest. There was a willingness to work which cheered her heart, but when Gladys saw the people seated before her, listening intently to her teaching about Christ and the Christian faith, she felt she was really doing the work God called her to do. From among the local salvationists she recommended some for training as officers to ensure future leaders.

Several years and many adventures later Gladys Calliss was transferred to the training college in Djakarta, Java. It seemed only right that she who knew the difficulties, but also the possibilities, of field operations, should be appointed to train men and women cadets. It was work she loved. Her tall, well-built form dwarfed the tiny Indonesians, but they were not afraid of her for she gave strong evidence of her love for them.

By now Indonesian came almost more readily to her tongue than English and she had adapted in every way to her second homeland. Eighteen years had passed since the raw missionary arrived with wonder in her eyes and deep dedication in her heart. Gladys knew that she was not the same person inwardly. Her faith in God had strengthened. She had matured.

Her capacity for slogging hard work, her dependability in all circumstances, her cheerful uncomplaining spirit, led to her being appointed in 1965 to the senior position of Chief Secretary for the whole of Indonesia, with colonel's rank. Now more problems than ever came to her desk, and her journeys took her further afield; yet she revelled in the opportunities of the position. Some of the children she had enrolled as junior soldiers became cadets and officers working under her direction. She officiated at their weddings, dedicated their babies, and mothered them all in the Lord.

Her level-headed administrative powers have been used to the full. In the beginning she faced many problems and disappointments due to national political instability, in a period during which lack of food and other commodities became irksome, but more recent progressive government policy has opened closed doors. With first-hand knowledge of the needs, she is able to direct policies and make decisions which have far-reaching consequences.

It brought her special joy when the Kulawi school in mid-Celebes, which she had helped to found, was re-built to accommodate primary children. There, too, temporary accommodation was provided for the first students to enrol in the teachers' training college. With Army schools in Indonesia now numbering eighty, teacher-training has become a necessity. There are many facets of importance to be watched and many daily problems to be met. All the queries come to Colonel Gladys's desk, but she has broad shoulders and can take them. On the medical side there are general and maternity hospitals, clinics and dispensaries. Eighty schools, numerous children's homes and two homes for the aged, plus ninety-five corps, come under her jurisdiction. All these she must visit, holding meetings and inspections. It is no sinecure.

Colonel Gladys Calliss is not troubled with the problem of knowing what to do with her free time for she has little of it. She has borne the burden of near-top leadership for eight years and as 1973 draws to its close she will enjoy some well-earned relaxation after twenty-six years in Indonesia, and then be ready for a new appointment. Her testimony is, 'Daily I thank God for my call, for health and strength, and for the privilege of service.'

CHAPTER SEVEN

The General's Furniture

SALVATION ARMY officers are nomads; single or married, they move from place to place as appointed by their leaders, and live in 'quarters'. These are houses or flats owned or rented by the Army, with basic furnishings supplied. One can always be sure of a bed, chair, crockery and cutlery. The rest, all the fancy and cosy additions which make a house into a home, are personal responsibility. It is quite a good idea! No Army family need carry furniture round or wonder what to do with Grandma's old heavy bedroom suite which she insisted on donating for the back room. The furniture and furnishings stay put. The people move. It is as simple as that.

But what discoveries await the new arrivals! Each member of the family reacts differently according to private interests.

Father announces rather pompously, 'I shall have to take the small bedroom for my study. There's no other place.'

Mother sighs, 'Those stairs will be heavy going and what a tiny kitchen! How shall I ever manage?'

The children race through the new rooms, opening cupboards and slamming doors until their exuberance takes them flying into the garden; there they subside into shy silence at the sight of the neighbour's children who will soon be their sworn friends.

An hour later Mother has located the cups and saucers and made a pot of tea, which she and Father sip thoughtfully while they survey the wallpaper, the curtains and the rugs, and decide where the radio will stand. Not once or twice but many times Army children have to face uprooting from their schools and friends and must learn to adapt to new circumstances and sometimes to new languages.

Early in life they learn that the furniture is the General's or the Army's, and that all basic requisites belong to headquarters. 'Tommy, don't kick that chair. You know it's the General's.' 'Mary, go easy with that tray. It's Army property.'

The same injunctions to carefulness are manifested all the way up the line of Army hierarchy. A salvationist visited the Army Mother when she lay dying of cancer. She recalls one small incident. Mrs. Booth asked her to pull up the blind and she did so somewhat energetically, only to hear from the invalid the gentle remonstrance, 'Careful, careful, my dear. That's Salvation Army property!'

An amusing but authentic anecdote is told of a four-year-old. Wise beyond his years, he knew that headquarters was the fountainhead of all supplies. He was proudly showing his new baby brother to a visitor. 'You know, we really wanted a baby *girl*,' he confided, 'but headquarters sent us another boy.'

So brave Army women refashion their homes time after time in many different places. Their treasured cushions and ornaments are brought out, a few photos here, a vase there, and soon the new quarters begin to feel like home.

But tastes differ very widely. The woman officer must pray for grace to live with loudly patterned curtains when she prefers plain soft colours, or with the mustard yellow of the stair-carpet that her predecessor chose because it looked bright and warm and could be obtained at a half-price sale.

'Simplicity for salvationists' was a theme often on the Army Mother's lips. Any supposed extravagance or fancy frill was frowned upon. When her eldest son Bramwell was to be married, she made herself responsible for the furnishing of the little home-to-be. Her impassioned adherence to utter simplicity and a spirit of unworldliness led her to have the mirrors removed from the bedroom wardrobe, as being too ostentatious. What the newly-weds thought about it is not left on record.

In the Army's early days self-denial was the keynote and austerity the melody for everyday living. But life was not gloomy. There was often a ring of joy about it, a gaiety that made light of the many deprivations, an acceptance of spartan living and financial stringency for the sake of the war against sin, for Jesus' sake.

There were, of course, times when the clouds hung low and the grim struggle to make ends meet loaded the spirit with heaviness. To tighten one's own belt and go without is easier than to deny the clamour of children for more to eat. Yet often in a remarkable way a neighbour would call with a loaf of freshly baked bread or a few eggs, and in an instant the darkness would lift and gratitude to God fill the heart with new courage and faith.

It was the children probably who most felt the scraping and the pinch to the point of resenting it. They had not 'laid their all on the altar' as had their parents and at times it was galling for them not to have what their school friends could afford. One lad, though, found that a chum from a rich home was tired of his daily sandwiches of ham and tongue and willingly exchanged them for the Army rations of slices of tomato or grated carrot. Fair exchange is said to be no robbery!

Religious phraseology and Army terms were imbibed by these children while they cut their milk teeth. The first games were of marches and meetings, with a cloth on a pole for the flag and two saucepan lids to bang together for the drum or cymbals. Dolls and teddies formed the audience and many a toddler has preached a fiery impromptu sermon, duly embellished with plenty of arm-waving, usually resulting in one of the dolls being helped forward to pray.

The present editor of the Swedish *War Cry*, Lt.-Colonel Karin Hartman, recounts how farewell orders came to her parents to move to Russia. She was only four at the time and her chief memory is that special bandoliers in the Russian colours of that era were sewn for the children to wear at the farewell gathering, to which occasion she therefore looked forward with keen anticipation.

Her mother, however, felt differently about taking a family of four young children into that unknown land. As she knelt by the side of a packing-case, laying in the children's clothes, tears rolled down her face. Her eleven-year-old son, bursting into the room, stared at her with astonishment, then blurted out, 'But, Mamma, aren't you on the altar?' The farewell orders were cancelled, for just then the Russian revolution broke out, but the query, 'Aren't you on the altar?' became a family byword when anyone baulked at a duty to be done.

Another officer-daughter recalls the humiliation she suffered as a schoolgirl, having to wear a cut-down from her father. His red jersey, having served his energetic person for a number of years, became frayed at the cuffs, so the sleeves were cut out to leave a pullover. When it was even more worn it was again cut down, this time to make a warm bodice for his daughter to wear under her frock. While she was fully dressed it did not matter, for she alone knew the guilty secret of the scarlet horror she carried about, but when the girls had to undress for gym, the poor child suffered agonies of mortification. She raced ahead of

the other girls to change first and, ironically, was always com-
mended by the teacher for being so quick!

How many new schools and unfamiliar textbooks the Army
children had to endure, complicated always by the inexplicable
yet implacably held local belief that the standard of education
in the new school was higher than that in the old, with the
foreseen insistence that the pupil must start in a lower class!
Before such a decision, parents were reduced to pleadings, at
times to tears, to no avail.

Sometimes a child had to start school in another country
without knowing the language. That was a problem with its
own pains, its own struggles, yet such children revealed the
magnificent powers of the human brain. Simply by listening to
the language and playing with other children, they acquired
facility much more quickly than their parents, who had to go
the hard way of the textbook. One Army family with several
children changed lands seven times in ten years, involving five
different languages.

The division of the class into Protestants or Roman Cath-
olics for religious instruction according to the parents' beliefs
brought bewilderment to one six-year-old. Running home she
queried, 'Mamma, when the Virgin Mary is a Catholic, how
can Jesus be a Protestant?'

It is quite natural that the Army which supplied the basic
necessities for the quarters of its officers should clearly mark
their ownership. We are indebted to Albert Orsborn, sixth
General of The Salvation Army, for a captivating account of
his childhood background:

Everything in our family life took the Army pattern. Three
times a day Army tunes were played by a musical clock. The
furnishings belonged to General Booth; a fact that became

quite menacing to the children when they stood on a chair, threw pillows, or danced on a bed. When we sat at table we saw the Army crest on the table-cloth and 'The Salvation Army' stamped on the cutlery.

When one said, 'Dad, what's the time?' father consulted, not a wrist-watch, but a large Victorian lever carried on a chain hitched to his braces and drawn from a capacious inner pocket. This time-piece was purchased at The Salvation Army Trade Department and carried the Army symbol and the text, 'My times are in Thy hand'. I seem also to remember a large red pocket handkerchief with a yellow crest on one corner.

When I went upstairs to bed carrying my lighted candle, I struck the light from a Salvation Army matchbox. This was the 'Darkest England' match. The Founder entered the match-making industry because he was incensed at the sickness and mortality rate in certain factories. He aimed at improving the lot of the workers.

Preparation for the weekend began on Friday night when a start was made on the bathing programme. We did not always have a bathroom; a tub in the kitchen had to suffice. Then there was a medicine parade: brimstone and treacle, or a vile concoction compounded by father, of rhubarb, sweet nitre and soda bi-carb. — a large spoonful of this or a pill, followed by a spoonful of jam.

And so to Sunday, which was entirely devoted to meetings. Before we boys commenced our religious exercises, we paraded for a hair-do. With a hot goffering iron mother made the waves which nature had denied us. Then with stiff starched Eton collars enclosing our rebel necks, we marched reluctantly to worship.*

* *The House of my Pilgrimage*, Salvationist Publishing and Supplies.

What courage and grit women have shown in making a home in the face of overwhelming difficulties! Think of the American, Elizabeth Brengle, appointed with her husband to Boston 1 corps in 1888. The living-quarters were just a small corner partitioned off from the meeting-hall, having as furnishings a smoky stove, a clothless table, a carpetless floor, and two or three rickety chairs. Night accommodation was provided by a bed in a corner curtained off by some yards of calico. The kitchen consisted of a shelf or two holding a few dishes and a gas-ring. The Brengles were educated people from good homes; moreover they had a little boy and a month-old baby, but they did not refuse the appointment. They cast themselves on God and did their best.

Before her marriage Elizabeth Brengle had led a leisurely pleasure-filled life. She was keen on sport, dancing, fashion and art. It was her love of skating which ruined the good health built up by life on her father's farm. Rosy-cheeked and hot with madcap skating in the cold, frosty air, she sat down panting to chat with friends and caught a chill which nearly cost her life. Her college studies had to be terminated and she remained in delicate health for the remainder of her life.

On a year's trip to Europe to visit art galleries and beauty spots, she met The Salvation Army and was intrigued by its teaching of holiness. Brought up as she had been in the Calvinistic faith, her gay-hearted fun would sometimes be swiftly followed by terrifying thoughts of death and judgment. Under Army influence she surrendered entirely to Christ and He became a living reality to her. She gave up visits to art galleries and began to study Army methods instead.

One day she was invited to visit Mrs. Catherine Booth in her home. The Army Mother received her in a rather shabby sitting-room, and quite casually drew out her work-basket and began to patch a grey flannel shirt. Surprise must have been registered in Elizabeth's face to see this great woman preacher engaged in so homely a task, but Mrs. Booth smiled and said, 'You won't mind if I go on with my work while we talk, will you?' The young visitor could not forget that incident. It showed so clearly that spartan living and simple manual work could go hand-in-hand with great intelligence gifts.

So in the small private space allotted to the Brengle family in the Boston hall, in drab and comfortless daily living, in poverty and hardship, Elizabeth tended her family and helped her husband in his pastoral duties.

In the street one day Samuel Brengle met two of his former professors and they ignored him. Worse was in store. A ruffian hurled a brick at his head and almost killed him. Months of convalescence produced his valuable book *Helps to Holiness*. Elizabeth's reaction to the painful incident was made with a paintbrush. One day Brengle found his wife painting a text on the brick which had nearly killed him. She had chosen, 'Ye meant it for evil, but God meant it for good'. And as Brengle himself pointed out, 'If there had been no little brick, there would have been no little book.'

*   *   *

Most Army homes today are equipped with reasonable comfort, but for officers on missionary service the change from one climate to another can be exhausting. To the missionary candidate, the future sphere of activity might seem to have something of the allure of a coloured postcard. Waving palms, tropical fruits, blue sky and glittering water are not the whole story. They convey neither the smells, stings, and dangers, nor the daily irritations of life in the tropics.

What must the young bride have felt whose honeymoon was

to be spent on Devil's Island? In 1933 The Salvation Army in France received permission, after impatiently waiting for a number of years, to commence operations in the penal settlement in French Guiana. Among the small group of officers chosen was a newly married couple. They exchanged Paris and their beloved France for the damp oppressive heat of Devil's Island, with its myriads of mosquitoes and giant hairy spiders. Yet these young officers not only survived but also raised a family in those unhappy surroundings, until in 1952 the Army flag which had waved its message of salvation over the colony was brought back to France by the last officer to return. The penal settlement had been abolished, largely owing to Salvation Army pressures.

It is sometimes asked whether the mother's involvement in pastoral work has any detrimental effect upon the children. Are they neglected for the sake of the Kingdom of Heaven? Catherine Booth felt strongly on that subject. It is told that 'her face would flush, her pulse become agitated, on listening to the charge against the Army that in making mothers preachers we disrupted the home and robbed the children of the mother's influence'. And Evangeline, her daughter, commented, 'Crowded as were my mother's days, never did she neglect her children, for whom she realised her particular responsibility.'

CHAPTER EIGHT

Anything . . . Anywhere

EACH young salvationist who applies for officership is given — to consider, pray over and complete — the Application for Training and Service as an Officer of The Salvation Army. The form contains many questions, one of which is: 'Are you willing to serve in whatever appointment you are given?'

Only a saint or a fool would unhesitatingly answer an immediate 'yes'. The normal person needs to consider the matter and weigh up possibilities. This is the crux of the inward battle for many young people. To serve God, yes; to serve people, yes; but to obey orders for the remainder of one's long, long life, to go where sent and do any kind of work . . . this is hard indeed. It is only made possible through a firmly held belief that behind Salvation Army authority stands God, who takes the threads of the everyday into His own hands and weaves them into the pattern He desires. Only in the light of that trust can the answer be 'yes'.

Another question on the form is equally searching: 'Are you willing, if required, to serve in another country?' The imagination immediately conjures up pictures of a hot climate with waving palms and dark-skinned people; a European land with a difficult language; the long, dark winters of the far north, iced in by snow and blizzards.

The young salvationist may find, during quiet prayer, that

texts come to the memory like, 'Go forth therefore and make all nations my disciples', and the refrain of the chorus, 'If Jesus goes with me I'll go . . . anywhere.' It was easy enough to sing, harder to be willing to put into practice. More prayer . . . then a written 'yes'.

For some salvationists the call to serve abroad comes early, haunting the quiet moments, edging up from the subconscious, giving nudges and urgings and pricks until suddenly there is a breakthrough: the challenge is faced and accepted.

Even stranger it seems when the person is a child. Matilda Hatcher was quite sure at nine years of age that God called her to take His good news to dark-skinned peoples. But her vicar in the village of Longstock, Hampshire, wasn't so sure. Even though Matilda had reached seventeen when she told him of her inward calling, he advised her to forget it. She was only a shepherd's daughter, one of ten children. She could take a missionary box and collect for missions. That would be enough.

The break for Matilda came in 1888 when she picked up a Salvation Army self-denial envelope in the street. She read of the need for money to support missionary enterprise; strong young women were required, who loved God and people, to work in the slums. Money Matilda didn't have. But she was young and strong. To the unknown Salvation Army she offered herself, only to meet another obstacle. She was considered too shy and retiring, too much the green country girl. Disappointment registered so unmistakably in her face that she was offered a trial year. She accepted it and remained with the Army for the rest of her life.

A few adventurous years followed her training in 1890. Matilda enjoyed the work in the slums, with its many-sided demands, sometimes dangerous to life and health. She learnt how to separate fighting women, how to stop a wife-beater, when to upbraid a recalcitrant youth and when to mother him. Above all, she learnt to love people, the outcasts, the wretchedly poor and destitute, and the unwanted children.

It was a *War Cry* which re-awakened the missionary call. Its caption proclaimed in large letters JAPAN FOR JESUS! Matilda knew her moment had come, but frustration met her again. Her medical certificate revealed that her health was not good enough for such an arduous venture. Despondently she pleaded, 'What does it matter what the doctor says? I may as well die in Japan as here.' Her fighting spirit brought victory, for William Booth recognised a kindred soul and accepted her.

Parting with her mother was not easy, but at least there were no tearful scenes. When Mrs. Hatcher was asked how she could allow her daughter to go so far away to an unknown land, she replied, 'I've always given a tenth of my money to God. Now He asks me for a tenth of my children, so of course she must go.'

The sea-voyage seemed endless, but on September 4th, 1895, the pioneer group of four salvationists landed in Tokyo, where high above the night mists the shining cone of Mount Fuji hung. They had arrived, but found they could not disembark until next day. They must first find some lodgings, preferably in the Japanese quarter of the city.

Next morning the four met for prayer. There was a special solemnity over the group. When they parted they would lay aside European clothes and assume Japanese dress. They had brought it with them, kimonos and sashes, with getas for their feet — wooden clogs held on by a strip between the toes. Their march through the city later that day seemed to cause amusement. They were covered with confusion to learn that the kimonos they had donned were customary night attire, not used by day! Back they went to European dress for ten days until more suitable garb could be found.

The first months had to be given to language study and meetings held with translators' help. The people seemed genuinely interested in the Army message and methods. One property owner was so impressed that he ordered his three hundred tenants to join the Army at once on pain of instant eviction. When it was explained to him that no such compulsion could be used in a matter of faith and belief, he capitulated, declaring himself willing to give them reasonable time to reflect and then, if they did not comply, he would raise their rents!

Captain Matilda Hatcher, progressing well with Japanese, was appointed to organise an inland corps about fifty miles from Tokyo. She described her new surroundings to her parents on three yards of decorated rice paper. The Japanese way of living mainly on rice and vegetables appealed to Matilda, but further progress with the language was more difficult.

In December 1896 she was transferred to Yokohama to open a Sailors' Home. There she met a new and terrifying experience on a day when the China Fleet was in port and breakfast at the Home was being served to a full house: four sausages and three eggs per man was considered a normal portion! Matilda described what occurred when the building was shaken by an earthquake.

Knives, forks and spoons cascaded to the floor. Plates crashed by the dozen. Rashers, sausages and eggs slithered on to the men's knees and bespattered their shirts. Overturned cups of scalding tea and hot coffee completed their discomfiture. Happily no lives were lost but every piece of china in the Home was broken.

Two officers from the flag-ship came to inspect the damage and the Army received a cheque from the admiral which enabled all the breakages to be made good.

One day a pastor approached Matilda, asking if she would help him with a baby to be christened. At a nearby brothel a woman had adopted a young child and wanted it baptised in church. Would Captain Hatcher make enquiries? Despite her comparative youth — she was only twenty-six years of age — Matilda had learnt in the school of slum service how to approach such a problem.

Rose, the proprietress of the brothel, was a beautiful young woman of striking appearance. She invited Matilda to tea with eight other girls, all elegantly gowned. After the meal the others left and Rose sat with the baby in her lap, looking for all the world like a madonna. The captain chose her words carefully, delicately probing to find out whose baby it was.

'It's mine!' insisted Rose passionately. Then the whole tragic story was revealed. A betrayed girl had been deserted in a port far away from her homeland, pregnant and alone. Rose had heard about her, had bought her child when it was born, and intended to bring it up as her own. She wanted to give it a good start by having it baptised in church. Matilda explained to her that to bring up a child properly she would have to move away from the brothel and live a different kind of life. Rose hesitated but at last accepted the condition for love of the child.

So the baptism was arranged. Matilda was to be the godmother. She never forgot the scene in the church that morning: herself in uniform carrying the baby, Rose walking beside her, haughty and beautiful, and behind them, two by two, the eight girls from the brothel in their best clothes.

When the chaplain asked Rose if she would renounce the devil and all his works, she hesitated and trembled. Fearful of the outcome, Matilda pressed the child into her arms, and hugging the little one hungrily to her breast, Rose responded firmly, 'I renounce them all.'

Rose kept her promise and gave up the brothel, taking a small cottage for herself and the baby, but only four years later the little one died. Matilda did her utmost to rouse the sorrowing Rose. The loss of her darling child, added to the toll of years of sinful living, sapped the mother's strength, and three months later Rose herself passed away.

In 1907 Matilda Hatcher was sent to China to prospect with Commissioner Railton the chances of commencing Army work, but it was not begun until eight years later. Instead the young officer was sent to India where for many years she was in charge of children's homes.

At fifty-two years of age, Lt.-Colonel Matilda Hatcher came to another surprising turn of the way. Her writing ability had been noticed and she was appointed to literary work at the London headquarters. She who had been out among people all her life now sat in an office and wielded a pen, but she wrote with that deep love and understanding which had characterised all her service. The books she wrote live, as the memory of Matilda Hatcher lives, with inspiration and blessing.

*   *   *

There are some people who seem stamped from childhood for God's service. They are apart by an invisible sealing of the Spirit of God. Such was Catherine Bannister. From a devout Church of England family, her father a solicitor, she started life well equipped with a good education. At sixteen she was converted. Later, a winter in London gave her an opportunity to hear Catherine Booth. The salvationists had come in from their march with bruised faces and torn clothing but radiant with joy and triumph. Mrs. Booth had preached on the difference between workers and *soldiers* of Jesus Christ. At the conclusion of the meeting Miss Bannister committed her life to active warfare against evil.

After training as an officer she was appointed to Tring corps. Already the uncomplaining manner in which she accepted frustrations showed her disciplined spirit. Neither furniture nor supplies had arrived in the little quarters but Catherine was resourceful. In her bag she carried a small saucepan and a little tea. Gathering a few shavings she boiled some water, added a little tea, and drank direct from the saucepan as soon as it had cooled sufficiently. Then rolling herself in her travelling-rug she lay on the bare boards to sleep. This was a foretaste of what she would endure as a missionary, for soon afterwards she was on her way to India where she received the significant name of *Yuddha Bai*, warrior sister.

From her sheltered home Catherine Bannister was thrown into the rough and harsh elements of pioneering in a foreign land. Heat, coarse native food, mosquitoes, language strain, all combined to damp the ardour of the new arrivals, but Catherine, in charge of the group, managed to rally their cooling courage.

The simplicity of Indian life appealed to her. One large room sufficed for sleeping, eating and studying. There was no furniture. The floor filled the purpose of bed, table and chair. She was soon leading meetings in the vernacular and would face a hostile Indian crowd unhesitatingly. Once when a sharp stone cut her face, she wiped away the blood with her sari and continued her message.

She was sent in charge of a district, to lead and inspire others in village evangelisation. From her pen we have a word picture of the 'Boom Marches' by which means the activities were expanded to other areas.

We lasses slept in a tent, the men mostly under the trees. We had two small carts for the luggage — bedding, cooking utensils, tent, drum, food and clothes. Each was allowed two blankets, one change of clothing, Bible and song book. Nothing else. But that was all we needed. Our food was of the coarsest but what did that matter? We had two cooked meals in the day. One at 11 a.m. consisting of rice, split peas and onions. The other about 3 p.m. of tea and chapatties, a sort of pancake. Our worst enemy was cold. Our hands and arms were cracked and bleeding at night, yet during the day it was scorching hot.

It had been Catherine Bannister's intention never again to leave India, but she was ordered to take a homeland furlough and on her return was sent in charge of another part of India.

Her glad and uncomplaining acceptance of spartan living was a byword among her colleagues who were — to speak the truth — a little afraid of this living apostle of poverty, with her lean figure and ascetic face. Yet as years passed the more tender side of Catherine's nature developed and she was never happier than when a tiny child cuddled up to her for a hug and a smile.

One of Catherine's closest women comrades almost feared to break the news that she was to be married. After a few silent moments Catherine warmly congratulated her and with unwonted frankness told how she had had to renounce earthly love to follow the path of duty, and what it had cost her. Catherine paved the way for the marriage with spontaneous generosity and even officiated herself at the wedding.

Returning to India for a third ten-year term of service, Colonel Catherine Bannister was found to have a malignant growth. The question of going back to England for an operation was raised but immediately scorned. Catherine was adamant. She would work as long as she could, then die in India. 'The Lord enticed me here,' she wrote, 'and I have never regretted it.' And in Indian soil she lies buried.

*   *   *

From India we turn to the former Belgian Congo to meet Major Ruth Siegfried in a typical setting.

She had arranged a strange object-lesson in the lecture hall of the Teachers' Training School in Kasangulu. The vase of flowers stood under the table, the cloth draped round it. On top of the table lay an unruly pile of objects — odd shoes, one brown, one black; a dirty basin; a soiled towel; a flat-iron.

The pupils filed in to evening prayers, their shining black faces registering astonishment as they glanced from the untidy table to the white-clad figure of the major seated at the organ, playing hymn tunes.

'My children, let me remind you of the good rule "A place for everything and everything in its place".' With these quiet words of reproach Ruth commenced evening prayers. Oh, that God would give her patience with her much-loved but often troublesome pupils!

After prayers one lad waited to speak to her. 'Mother, why is it that even when we understand what you teach us about order, we cannot follow it? Why is there this gulf between knowing and doing?'

The white officer was startled by the understanding of the black lad before her, his questing gaze on her face. *This gulf between knowing and doing . . .* could anyone better express the age-long conflict of mankind?

Back in her own house in the school settlement, Ruth Siegfried marvelled once more at the flashes of spiritual and moral insight of her pupils, seizing upon every small sign of progress to strengthen her faith in the task to which God had called her: the education of Congolese youth to a teaching grade.

Ruth Siegfried was to give three terms of service in the former Belgian Congo. In 1935 she had felt that mysterious call which God lays upon some of His children and she had obeyed. In a way, she had always known that she would be a missionary and had always presumed that it would be among black people. Born in Alsace of three generations of Lutheran pastors, Ruth was brought up with strict and narrow discipline. With the purpose of 'renouncing the world', even harmless amusements were banned and books of fiction were forbidden. Attendance at church on Sunday was compulsory, as well as at daily family prayers. Each of the six Siegfried children had to spend some time in Bible-reading and prayer each morning. There was no avenue of escape, at least physically. What Ruth did was to use part of the time on her knees to look over her school lessons for the day.

The word 'conversion' was so often dinned into her ears that she came to hate it. Mamma, pure and ardent in her faith, told her girls that it was the only thing that she desired in their lives — that, and that they should be 'kept from the world'. What was this world that they must be shielded from? Ruth didn't really know. She knew she was forbidden to go on the roundabouts at the fair. Were they 'the world'?

Papa was different. He never mentioned conversion in the home. He would play chorales on an old harmonium and Ruth would sing, putting her whole soul into the beloved German words. When Papa put on his pastor's robes he became a being apart, sacred, remote and untouchable. With her whole being Ruth vibrated and responded to the liturgy of her church.

On the eve of her confirmation she slipped into the little summer-house at the end of the garden and knelt to consecrate herself to God and His service. The next day, in solemn joy, she felt her father's hands placed on her head and heard his warm voice recite her favourite text: 'Rejoice, because your names are written in heaven.'

A few months later Ruth attended some missionary-meetings. When the collection plate was passed round, realising that she had nothing to give, she scribbled a few words in pencil and laid the note on the plate. She had written, 'I give myself.'

This did not mean that all her spiritual seeking had ceased. Ruth was too sincere, too honest a soul, to be able to accept her parents' religion as her own. She must find God for herself. She must touch reality. She began teaching. In the evenings she took organ and singing lessons. One night in 1931 she attended a park concert in Strasbourg. When the last strains of the orchestra died away, she looked for a tram, but the conviction seized her that she must return to the park to find God. Thus it was that a park-keeper found her kneeling beside a bench at midnight.

'What are you doing here?' he asked roughly.

'I'm waiting,' she replied.

'Is he still in the pub?'

'No, I'm waiting for God. I want to know if there is a God. If He does exist, I'll serve Him wholly.'

'Bah!' replied the park-keeper. 'Christians are no better than other people.'

'But salvationists then?' Ruth had been to some of their meetings.

'Ah, they're different. They put their religion into practice.'

Suddenly a flood of joy and certainty welled up in Ruth's heart though she could hardly explain why. She had found her way. The next step was clear.

'Here,' she cried to the park-keeper, pressing her New Testament upon him, 'take this, I've been seeking and now I've found certainty. Start to seek, too.'

Too astounded to refuse, he accepted the New Testament and Ruth, radiant with the assurance of God's acceptance of her life, returned home. Twelve months later she was a cadet in The Salvation Army's training college in Paris, in preparation for a teaching ministry in the Congo.

The inner problems of pioneering overseas soon met Ruth. Added to climatic difficulties was the single-handed supervision of a school with nearly three hundred pupils. True, she had a house-boy to cook and clean for her, but she shuddered to see him polish his shoes with the tea-towel or — worse still — wipe the dishes with his loin-cloth! The soul of good order, Ruth tried to train him in small daily duties such as sprinkling the floor with water *before* he swept it. It was useless. As often as not he swept first and sprinkled after. Then she would ask him, 'What do you need today for housekeeping?' 'Nothing, nothing at all,' his smiling face would assure her. An hour later he would want money for charcoal for the hot iron; at midday he needed money for soap; during the afternoon he would find there were no biscuits; by evening he had run out of flour.

Ruth's bed was elegantly draped with a mosquito net, but once away from it she could be attacked from all quarters at once. White ants ate their way through the cement floor under her bookshelves, so she had to re-arrange the furniture and paint the corners of the room with tar. Wet through with sweat several times a day, she felt her strength sucked out of her. Congo wild life for her did not consist of tigers and leopards, but of pesky and unavoidable creatures such as cockroaches two inches long, ants, centipedes, lizards and spiders.

These home trials, though irritating, were not the heaviest burden of her service. Responsive to God with every fibre of her being, she had thrown herself without reserve into the wonderful opportunities before her to bring both education and knowledge of God to hundreds of Congo youth. 'Without reserve' — the wholesale giving of herself was to be both the glory and the undoing of her service. Her health began to fail. Blinded by headaches, weary both physically and mentally, Ruth would force herself to take her classes, to attend to all other duties, even when her spirit drooped within her. Another element sapped her vitality — the thoughtless way in which her pupils pressed their demands upon her. 'Are you already tired in God's service?' they would ask. Yes, Ruth was tired, unutterably tired. But homeland furlough was approaching, when the taut strings could slacken and the weary mind and body find relief.

In 1946 she wrote to her father:

My stay in the Congo has been a time of passionate, incessant, satisfying activity. Sometimes I have thought that the loveliest thing that could happen would be to bleed to death out of pure love for Africa. As long as one loves, one lives nobly. Helping others to climb one grows in stature. That is why a fire burns within me. If my inner life dries up, all my missionary work becomes soulless . . . becomes just an eccentric way of life. But it is easier to walk on the edge of a knifeblade than to live out integral Christianity here.

Poor Ruth! Conscientious, painstaking to a fault, sincere and thorough, she could never easily accept laziness and dishonesty among her pupils. And now a new element of unrest appeared. The fourth form went on strike, demanding to be promoted to the fifth form, to be given another classroom, other textbooks, another monitor, and so on *ad infinitum*. The strike spread to the whole Central School, and when the bell rang the next morning, not a single boy appeared in class. In addition they vowed they would march the twenty-five miles to Leopoldville (now Kinshasa) to make their complaints.

Knowing that the worst punishment one can inflict on an African boy is to stop his food, Ruth announced that she herself would fast until the boys returned to school. Only in this way did she feel that she could bring them to reason. Even while she spoke the fourth-formers were starting their long trek to the capital to make official complaint against their headmistress.

Ruth's fast lasted seventy-two hours. With her physical weakness and tense nerves, it seemed like an eternity. Finally the boys came back. Youngsters hurled themselves down the hill to meet them. 'Hurry! Go quickly to mother or she will die!'

The whole fourth form gathered round the headmistress's little bungalow. Through the open door they shouted, 'Forgive us, please. We will never do it again!' And in a weak voice Ruth replied, 'I hope you won't. My fast has wiped out your guilt. There will be no punishment. Tomorrow we will resume lessons again.'

Major Siegfried's third period in the Congo was drawing to a close, but before returning to her homeland she was to have the great joy of seeing all her pupils in the teachers' training course pass their examinations. As the final days approached she pleaded with them to put matters right between their souls and God. They would be going out into the bush with sole responsibility for a village school. They would need to feel the presence of God's Spirit with them. No evil thing must come between them and God.

'Look,' she said to them. 'Let everything be put straight before you leave this place. If you have anything to confess, write it on a piece of paper and put it into this basket. Then the joy of the Lord can be your strength, and I will dedicate you to your new tasks.'

Gathering up the fragments of paper at the end of the meeting, she returned to her house, her pathway lit by the brilliant stars hanging low in the tropical sky. Behind her she heard quick running footsteps. It was N . . .

'Mother, the joy doesn't come through to me.'

Major Siegfried looked through the little notes in her hand, found the right one and read, 'I cheated in one test.'

'Take this match, N . . . We are going to burn this paper. See, it is only ashes now. That is how God treats our sins when we confess them. He effaces them. Blots them right out. Are you happier now?'

N . . . was radiant.

Together they knelt. 'Help me, Lord,' the young man prayed, 'not to waste my youth. I don't want to be good only when I am old. Accept my life today. I want to show my people what love is capable of doing, which is what our mother has done for us.'

And with the blessing of their mother resting over them the new village teachers were sent to their first school appointments.

Ruth Siegfried, now with brigadier's rank, spends her retirement in Paris, but her heart is ever warm for her beloved Congolese pupils.

*　　　*　　　*

Another woman who has given exceptional service, in the field of missionary education is Lt.-Colonel Anna Beek, B.A., B.Ed., of South Africa. She came into contact with The Salvation Army in her home, the Netherlands, being greatly impressed by the quality of life of some officers she had met. She regarded them as saints of this modern world.

Anna Beek had obtained her teacher's diploma as well as a diploma in social service in Amsterdam before completing her Salvation Army training in 1936. Two years later she offered for missionary work among the coloured people of South Africa. After a term in evangelical centres she obtained her degree of B.Ed. from the University of Johannesburg and was appointed headmistress of the Fred Clark Institute, situated in the middle of an area where a hundred and seventy thousand detribalised Bantu live. This was the kind of service she had envisaged for her life: teaching and training coloured people.

As the Institute progressed and expanded, she felt the advisability of qualifying still further for her position as headmistress. In 1955 she was accepted for further studies in Brussels, Belgium, and emerged a year later with the diploma of the Colonial School.

In increasing measure Anna Beek was equipping herself for educational work and giving all her time and energy to that cause. Her learning capacity is phenomenal. She speaks fluent Dutch, English, French, Afrikaans and Lingala. In addition, she has outstanding spiritual qualities and wields a powerful influence upon those working with her, as well as upon her students. She could well be called God's impecunious saint, for she never has any money left to spend on herself. There is a continual giving to help this student with books, that one with his fees, or another to visit his family. Anna Beek is the personification of self-giving and self-denial.

In 1957 came a change of scene, when she was appointed principal of the Kinshasa Secondary School, Zaïre (former Belgian Congo), with six hundred students. Once again by her personal example and integrity she commanded the loyalty and respect of the staff and the deep affection of her students. During the political upheaval a group of indigenous leaders visited the school. It was at a time when missionaries were being sent home and fears were entertained that the Principal would be involved. She was called out from her class for interrogation. Immediately her older pupils flocked round her and as a close and living body-guard they accompanied her to the questioning. A few minutes later she was sent back to class. The danger was over.

The pull of the coloured people of South Africa was still strong upon Anna Beek, and when her term in Zaïre was completed she returned to the Fred Clark Institute and Training College for the Bantu folk, with the rank of Lt.-Colonel.

The Institute had developed considerably in her absence and as Secretary for Education and Literary Affairs, she found she had a full-time job. She had an innate genius for organisation, for once she had settled into a position the wheels began to whirr effectively and soon the various branches of the programme were extended. Only a person with the complete devotion to duty which characterises Lt.-Colonel Beek could have maintained the pace of her many commitments.

In 1970 this woman of outstanding ability, yet with a tender, compassionate heart, was appointed principal of the European Training College in Johannesburg, while retaining her office as Secretary for Education and Literary Affairs in the whole of South Africa. Her call to that land led her into a rich and satisfying life which she has never regretted.

CHAPTER NINE

Officer-Doctors and Nurses

AMONG Salvation Army officer-doctors who have given their specialised service in relieving pain and sickness are several women. First to be named among them — for she was something of a twentieth-century saint — is one who came from a different race and culture from our own. Rin Iwasa, born in 1891, was one of eleven children in an aristocratic Japanese family. Their parents, followers of the Buddhist–Shintoist philosophy, determined that each child should have the best possible education.

Rin had a brilliant mind and graduated when still only fifteen. She was no blue-stocking, though. She learned the traditional arts of cultured Japanese women, which included flower arrangements, the tea ceremony and brush writing. Full of energy, she excelled in folk-dancing and was a popular partner in sports. Through reading the life of Florence Nightingale the young Japanese student decided to enter Tokyo Medical School. Among the teaching professors was Dr. Sanya Matsudo.

Dr. Matsudo was already a convinced Christian when William Booth first visited Japan in 1907. He found his heart warming to the impassioned challenge of the Founder for loving, caring service to the very poor. These, unable to pay fees for medical service, simply died in their homes in pain and neglect, so the salvationists reported.

That plea of the Founder was remembered when he died in 1912, and a hospital for the sick poor was deemed Japan's most suitable memorial to him. Gifts poured in from all classes of the people. The royal family donated a hall which had been specially built to accommodate visitors to a state funeral. It became the reception hall of the Hospital for the Poor, the other buildings being grouped around it. As the hospital's walls were being raised The Salvation Army sought for a medical man qualified by his skill, but also by his compassion, to become its superintendent. There were public appeals for applicants for the post.

It stirred the whole medical world when Dr. Sanya Matsudo gave up his extensive practice with its high income to pioneer the free medical service to Tokyo's poor. Matsudo, throwing himself with all his energy and enthusiasm into the new task, took an even further step. He became a salvationist. In his lectures he emphasised the necessity of a good character and high ideals in medical men and women, and his life spelt out the truth of his words. This one Christian among the thirty instructors was used by God to grip the minds and hearts of the students. Numbers of them visited him in his home to hear more. And one of these was Rin Iwasa, avid to learn about the Christian religion which he followed. She asked questions, discussed and borrowed books on Christianity and The Salvation Army. It was all so bafflingly new to her, yet it appealed.

Two months after Rin took her degree, becoming one of Japan's first women doctors, she made her decision to join Dr. Matsudo's staff. She would become his assistant. Her parents were horrified and Rin's sensitive heart suffered days of agony, but she held firm. She intended to serve the poor and outcast.

The Hospital for the Poor not only received the sick who

came: doctors and nurses went out into the slums of Tokyo to find ailing people and bring them into loving care. This brought the new doctor into a world of harsh reality which she had never really imagined. Behind her lay a comfortable, shielded home. What could she know of abject poverty, filth, rampant disease, and their accompanying smells? One day two mothers came to the hospital with tiny ones strapped to their backs. One baby was already dead, the other nearly so. Both had measles. It was the vanguard of a fearful epidemic which took the lives of many undernourished little ones. Dr. Iwasa went herself to check conditions in the district.

She found a windowless hovel sheltering eighteen people. By flashlamp in the foetid atmosphere she made a hasty examination. They were all seriously ill, but had had no medical help. Four siblings of the dead baby had perished in that very room. In a neighbouring barrack-like building sixty-one families were squeezed together almost without ventilation or sanitation.

It became clear to Dr. Iwasa, however, that the biggest scourge among the people was tuberculosis. Japan's total loss of life through typhoons, earthquake, fire and flood was topped at that time by the devastating losses through that disease. The Army's General Hospital was already too small. What was needed was a sanatorium, dedicated to patients unable to pay any fees.

At this time Rin was invited to join a party of delegates to The Salvation Army congress held in London. On the voyage she had a moment of illumination, an awareness of God's hand on her life, guiding her into further involvement with the Army. At the close of the congress Rin remained in London to be trained as a Salvation Army officer.

She returned to Japan in 1915 as a captain. The world was

at war. Her parents were still heartsore over her Christian loyalties, but Rin had her work and also God's assurance that she was in her right place. She was Dr. Matsudo's first assistant, with two hundred poor patients under her care. But Rin was more than their doctor. She was also their minister. She spoke so easily of God and His goodness as she went about her daily duties. A number of conversions resulted. She held prayers with both staff and patients, and with the families which camped round the hospital.

In 1930 the saintly Dr. Matsudo died of the same disease he had striven to cure in others. Dr. Rin Iwasa became his successor, although this was quite an extraordinary position for a woman in the Japan of that day. With great courage she faced the heavier demands made upon her. Dr. Matsudo had discussed plans for the future with her and these she began to introduce, such a physiotherapy and the colony system. He had also cherished the hope of building another sanatorium, as the first was now cramped for space. One morning Dr. Iwasa took her staff to a pine-clad area on the outskirts of Tokyo and asked them to kneel with her and claim the site for a second sanatorium. The building was started in 1933.

Rin Iwasa was also a competent business woman. She combined work-therapy with healthy exercise and good diet by surrounding the hospital with vegetable gardens and chicken runs, where convalescing patients could spend profitable hours. Professional men from all over Japan, trying to discover the secret of the woman-doctor's success in conquering tuberculosis, came, saw and noted down the treatment used, but they realised soon that there was more to it than that. The faith of the salvationist was making her patients hopeful and harmonious, by giving them knowledge of a God who loved them and cared about them.

The Second World War menaced the scene and The Salvation Army in Japan was dissolved by decree. Both its sanatoria were taken over by the Government, but Dr. Iwasa was ordered to continue as chief medical officer for the four hundred patients and one hundred staff. For her contribution to social welfare work the doctor received in 1944 the Emperor's Order of the Blue Ribbon.

During the period of the war Dr. Rin Iwasa was a bastion of strength to the former Japanese officers of the liquidated Salvation Army. No uniform could be worn, no meetings held, but in twos and threes they could unite to pray together, fanning each other's faith that one day they would be able to resume their vocations. In a few minutes snatched from her many duties Dr. Iwasa gave them words of counsel and encouragement, and occasionally she shared a little food or money with those who were most needy. The strength of her influence was seen when the war ended. Two hundred Japanese men and women who had been pre-war Salvation Army officers joined in sending an historic cable to international headquarters in London, asking for the re-establishment of the Army in their land.

In 1946 the re-formed Salvation Army was honoured when Lt.-Colonel (Dr.) Rin Iwasa received a summons to lecture to the Emperor and Empress on the cure of tuberculosis.

Natural disasters frequently occur in Japan and from time to time relief operations have to be on a large scale. This was the case with the flood which devastated vast areas of the Kwanto plain just outside Tokyo in 1948. Dr. Iwasa herself led a medical team to bring succour to the many wounded and destitute. Such a strenuous life took toll of her health, but even after she withdrew from active medical work, she still conducted the business affairs of the two sanatoria from her bed. And it was from that bed in her own hospital that she was, in Army terminology, 'Promoted to Glory'.

* * *

An officer-doctor pair are Colonel Daniel and Mrs. Sölvi Andersen, both of them of Norwegian parentage. Dr. Mrs. Andersen, M.B., B.Ch. (Oslo), as Sölvi Hammer, had qualified as a doctor in Norway before she offered herself to The Salvation Army as a missionary. During her medical studies in Oslo, Sölvi made a personal commitment of her life to God and she joined with other Christian students in regular prayer meetings. As the attendance at these increased, it was felt that a more definite evangelical approach should be followed among fellow-students. This led to the commencement of the Medical Students' Christian Union, of which Sölvi was a founder-member. This has grown so vigorously that in 1973 it counts more than half of the first-year students as members. Surely this is the record for Europe's medical schools? When Dr. and Mrs. Andersen visited Oslo in 1972 for a medical missionary conference, more than one hundred doctors and students attended.

During an obligatory pause in her medical training due to lack of openings in Norway, Sölvi came to London and took her midwifery examination at the Army's Mothers' Hospital, Clapton. While in London she met a Norwegian salvationist just qualifying as a surgeon and the two had quite naturally many mutual interests. Separately, each felt called to become a Salvation Army officer and, with their degrees assured, they entered the London Training College.

When Sölvi became first a doctor then an Army officer, she reckoned it equivalent to taking the veil, as far as marriage was concerned, and had pushed that possibility out of her thoughts. Even her friendship with the young surgeon with roots in her own northern land, who was also destined for the mission field, did not prepare her for the glad surprise of being loved and ardently courted. The veil had not been so irrevocably taken, and in the autumn of 1938 the two were married in Norway. Soon afterwards they were embarking for India.

The Indian chapter of their lives was to be an extended one, stretching in all over twenty-one years. They were appointed to Ahmednagar, where the disused hospital had been bought by The Salvation Army. It had lain neglected for eight years, so dust lay everywhere and some of the instruments had rusted. The first job was spring-cleaning; it lasted two to three months, but the news that the doctors had come soon spread, and patients began to arrive.

Between them the surgeon and the doctor had one trained nurse whose ministrations they must share. When the surgeon operated the doctor had to assist him as operation-nurse. It was mostly minor surgery and maternity cases at first, with the usual skin diseases, sore eyes and malnutrition. One woman came in advanced labour and was found to have cholera, the first case of that disease that Sölvi had ever seen. But she pulled both mother and baby through, without an epidemic starting. Life began to get hectic, for Sölvi, busy visiting dispensaries in surrounding villages where out-patients would cluster like flies, scattering a little as the doctor arrived, then patiently waiting in a solid block for the attention she could give them, was expecting her own first child.

Baby Andersen now joined the treks in the bullock cart around the village dispensaries, as did the succeeding three children in their turn. In between seeing patients, the mother had to feed and bath the little ones, but through precautions taken and the protecting care of God no baleful disease was ever contracted.

Before the birth of one of her babies, Dr. Sölvi was not able to relax her heavy programme at all, for her husband was away at a conference, leaving her in charge. Two hours before her own child was born she was delivering another woman of her baby. But all went well, with the help of a woman doctor from a neighbouring mission.

Plans for a nurses' training school were made, because it was seen as an absolute essential, and an application to the Government was approved. The start was inauspicious, in a basement approached by some dark steps. A visiting British surgeon general said as he walked down them, 'This is a rum hole!' but he found a well-equipped classroom at the bottom. The wife of the Governor, Lady Coleville, gave active interest and support and soon plans for a worthy building were in hand. India's first woman architect helped to design the Nurses' Training School.

It meant, of course, extra work for Dr. Daniel Andersen and Dr. Sölvi, both of whom had to make time to give lectures. The Andersens were missionary officers, which meant that their interests lay not only in the medical field but also in evangelism. Among the student-nurses and the cleaning-staff they started Bible classes. Most of the nurse-trainees had registered as Christians but that simply indicated their caste, and their parents' beliefs, and not their own personal commitment. The hospital cleaners and general helpers came from the lower castes and were illiterate, so the Andersens started adult literacy classes for them. One of the men technicians slightly startled Dr. Sölvi when he asked about 'the adultery classes'!

One great problem for Dr. Sölvi was the male dominance in the families. It was always the husband who told the doctor what was wrong with his wife, describing her pains and fears while she stood with downcast eyes. Sölvi would cut him short, saying, 'I want to examine your wife,' and with a firm hand on his shoulder she would propel him towards the door while he loudly protested that he was the husband and had a right to stay. But out he went! Then Dr. Sölvi turned kindly to the rather frightened woman, questioning her, reassuring her, and examining her.

Emphasis on major surgery and the gradual build-up of the nursing staff enabled more patients to be treated. In the area around the hospital there was a population of about a million people. The war years brought an additional fifteen thousand Indian soldiers to the town and Dr. Sölvi was asked by the military authorities to visit the wives and children each week in the three large camps.

Many patients came by bullock cart, or even on foot, from up to fifty miles away, accompanied by the usual muster of half a dozen relatives, with mother-in-law in charge of them all. The doctor had to use her sternest voice to get these relatives out of the wards at night. Once she found a man in one of the beds in a woman's ward.

'Who are you and where is the patient?' she demanded.

'I'm the husband and the patient is my wife, sleeping under the bed,' was the surprising answer. The doctor knew how to tackle that situation and the man withdrew in a hurry, leaving his sick wife to creep into the vacated bed.

An American hospital functioning some distance away was for a time without a doctor, so Sölvi took her five-month-old baby with her and spent six weeks in the village to attend to urgent cases. Late one evening a message came asking her to come to a dying girl. It meant several miles of travelling in the rough, unsprung bullock cart over stony roads in the pitch dark.

When she arrived at the hut she found a teenage girl in a fit of hysterics. Dr. Sölvi splashed her liberally with cold water and the 'dying' girl miraculously recovered. The village head-man — rather ashamed at having brought the memsahib doctor such a long night journey for so little — compensated by rous-ing half the village and presenting them for examination. Next morning a very tired doctor endured the jolting bullock cart back to her dispensary.

Dr. Daniel and Dr. Sölvi Andersen returned to London in 1960, but they regard their long service in India as being the most satisfying part of their life, when their missionary call received rich fulfilment.

* * *

Nursing in a modern hospital in the western world is totally different from district nursing in undeveloped countries. Ap-titude, devotion to duty, and compassion, are required in both spheres, but on the more primitive field one can be faced with sudden emergencies which have to be met single-handed with one's own resources.

A woman who became a legend in her lifetime is Mary Styles of Queenstown, whose name is associated with the Venda people near the northern border of South Africa. Her first ap-pointment as lieutenant from the Training College in Johan-nesburg in 1929 plunged her into such a new world of exciting and frightening daily happenings, that only a young woman of great inward strength could have withstood it.

Vendaland is remote from civilisation and the new lieutenant had plenty of time during the long smoky train journey to feel apprehensive. It was hardly any relief to exchange the hard train-seat for the dilapidated bus crowded with people, which bumped and jolted along dirt- and mud-tracks for what seemed endless hours. The tropical bush hid almost all views, but Mary caught a glimpse of two raging rivers that they crossed. Finally they drew up at a plain stone building almost hidden in dense undergrowth. It was the Army Settlement and Mary was made welcome, and later initiated into the primitive form of life that would be hers for years to come.

The Salvation Army Training College curriculum did not include much that Mary now found she was expected to do. She had to start by clearing away the undergrowth, cutting down weeds and wrestling with bushes with strong obdurate roots.

She watched the way the district nurse handled cases until she herself could adjust a bandage, clean up a wound, wash a new-born baby or bury a dead body. In addition to holding meetings for the country people she had to learn to dress croco-dile bites, pull out an aching tooth, or cope with a mishandled birth. Following primitive tribal customs, a woman in difficult labour was laid on a bed of cow-dung and sluiced with buckets of cold water! Tactfully Mary had to introduce more humane practices. The district included both mountains and swamps, bush and arid plain, swollen rivers and dry water-courses, with plenty of wild life visible by day and audible by night.

Mary's resourcefulness led sometimes to humorous, though unfortunate, experiences. Lack of space was a problem, so she decided to make bricks in order to build. By toiling long hours in the heat she and her colleague achieved a huge pile of twenty-five thousand unbaked mud bricks. Then came the rains, earlier than usual. When the storm ceased Mary went out to find a massive mound of dripping red clay— all that re-mained of their efforts! They confessed ruefully to each other that what they needed was 'know-how'. Borrowing a do-it-yourself book, they found out how to construct a kiln. Then once more they tackled brick-making, this time baking each batch as it was ready, until once again they had the large quota required. Those bricks withstood many rainstorms.

The ladies also managed to dig a well and zinc-line a water-tank. Then in expansive mood they decided that the time had come for the erection of a lean-to which would house a much-needed bathroom and a pigsty. It was unfortunate that Mary decided to try out the amenities of the bathroom just when the wind was blowing up. It came in storm-gusts and proved too strong for the new walls. The bathroom collapsed and so did the pig-sty! Poor Mary had to chase the pig through the under-growth, for they needed it. She had been told that the fat of a pig mixed with caustic soda would produce enough soap to last for two years so she could not afford to lose her supply. Frantic attempts were made to catch the errant animal and finally it was tethered with a rope where the sty had once been.

Mary Styles worked for eight years in this demanding area, serving as untrained nurse, midwife, teacher and dentist. Once when she had travelled thirty miles into the bush by mule cart, she allowed the tired animals a drink. The water must have been poisoned for the mules died, leaving the young woman a long way from home with a mule-less cart for company.

Then came a welcome break for her. She was to return to Durban to train as nurse and midwife. Practice she had had in plenty; now she would have both theory and practice in the antiseptic atmosphere of a hospital.

She enjoyed hospital life and routine, and the prospect of returning to the hardships of Vendaland was unwelcome. It is always harder for the seasoned missionary to face what she knows lies ahead than for the novice to launch out on the adventure of the unknown. Mary Style chose the difficult way for love of Christ and the Venda people. How they welcomed her back! True, time had seemed to stand still while she was away. There were the same primitive huts to crawl into, where women had to be delivered in a dense smoky atmosphere, with interested relatives crowding round. But now Mary was better qualified to help them. In time the settlement became a group of square concrete buildings with office, clinic-corps and living-quarters. The maternity wing had only nine beds, but as the mothers stayed only two days after the birth, there was a constant intake of new patients.

With the expansion came the need for a larger store-room. Mary was now an experienced builder, not only with mud bricks but also with concrete blocks that she made herself. When asked when she found the time she laughingly replied, 'In the early hours of the morning when there's nobody about to ask questions.' The donation of a fully equipped ambulance added a very distinctive and modern touch to the clinic, but the trolley-stretcher designed for city transport simply collapsed on the stones and mud of the Venda roads. Never mind! Mary had her own invention: a large sack with holes cut in the corners and stout branches thrust through. That primitive stretcher took the strain of both the up- and down-grades on the mountain paths.

One day a two-pound premature baby was brought to Mary. The family had rolled it in an old flour bag and flung it on the dung-heap to die. When Mary stripped the cloth from the living mite, she found it a seething mass of red ants. In a warm bath she dislodged them and soothed the baby while it died. It was a small incident but significant of her loving care for the most helpless of the Venda people.

For more than twenty-five years Mary served them. In a farewell tribute to her in 1970, the commissioner general for the Venda and Tsonga ethnic groups wrote:

In the darkest moments of the lives of many Venda, Brigadier Styles was there to save, to nurse and to serve. Through
this work she has built for herself a lasting monument in the
hearts of the Venda.

*   *   *

To serve as a nurse in the highlands of New Guinea was the
dream of Dorothy Elphick, a young New Zealand nurse. She
had become a Salvation Army officer. Now the attraction of
pioneering, and of hardships to be conquered, difficulties to be
met and overcome, filled her soul as the way opened up.

The New Guinea highlands in 1958 provided an almost
Stone Age environment. Narrow, unmade roads, rickety
bridges, muddy bogs, tortuous mountain paths and icy winds
were but the background to other difficulties. Age-old super-
stition, tribal malpractices, primitive living in squalid surroundings, malnutrition through ignorance — these stood
almost like a thick stone wall against any attempt to help the
people medically.

For three years from 1966 Captain Elphick took charge of a
government rural health centre of thirty beds and twelve medi-
cal-aid posts, serving a population of thirty-five thousand. It
was strenuous and taxing.

The urge to pioneer was still strong in Dorothy Elphick's
heart, not a whit quenched by all she already faced. In May
1970 she set out to explore the Gimi area of the Papua-New
Guinea region, to consider possible centres of activity. With her
old car loaded with camping gear she set out alone, although
some of the tribes in the district were known to be cannibals.

Leaving her car at a New Tribes mission station Dorothy
walked on for three hours to a Gimi village called Misapi. In
the evening the men gathered to talk to her. They had marked a

piece of land for a place of worship. They hungered for the Gospel. How that gladdened Dorothy's heart! She had not told them she was a nurse. All they knew was that she was a Salvation Army officer, a bearer of the good news of God's salvation. They wanted her for that reason.

In the next few days she explored other villages, up slippery mud slopes where a boy had to cut steps for her with a spade and two others pull her up. A line of small boys followed with her kitbag, lamp, kettle and hold-all. A sick woman brought up the rear of the procession. What a pity that a film camera could not have covered that eventful journey! Next day she was out alone exploring, still on slippery tracks through the bush, picking swollen leeches off her bare legs and feet, walking through the cloud and mists of the highlands to the home of another lone woman missionary. The trek lasted over ten hours and on arrival Dorothy was too exhausted to do more than wash and tumble into bed.

On receipt of Captain Elphick's report, the Army authorities decided to open a centre in Misapi. When she arrived back she let word drop of her nursing qualifications and a village shop was lent her as a temporary clinic. She herself lived in a grass-roofed hut with earthen floor, slept on a camp bed, cooked on an open fire, and washed in a baby's bath. She was all of forty miles of mountainous road away from the nearest doctor.

The site allotted to Captain Elphick for her future clinic was covered with reeds ten feet high, and volunteers were asked to help clear it with a minimum of hand-tools. It was a back-breaking task. Then a fence had to be built round the site to keep out foraging pigs. When the project is completed there will be a clinic, a ward, a house for the captain and a hall for worship. Dorothy smiles to herself as she treats the queue of sick villagers waiting for attention after the morning prayers she has conducted with them. Has her inward urge for pioneering now been satisfied? Perhaps . . . for a few years.

*   *   *

Another nursing sister who always seems to hit the trouble spots of the earth is Major Eva den Hartog of the Netherlands. What that woman has experienced would alone fill a book. During her training as a nurse she read an article in the Dutch *War Cry* about the need on the missionary sectors. Without hesitation she contacted Salvation Army headquarters in Amsterdam and offered herself for training. She received her officer's commission in 1948.

Watch her first in the Congo, now Zaïre, where she spent three service periods. Matured by experience, she summed up each situation with sober, factual eyes and astonishing control. With a mobile dispensary she toured the jungle districts round Kinshasa. It was 1965 and there were as yet no clinics built, so Eva, with a Congolese male nurse and two helpers, had to work in the open under the shade of palm trees or in a borrowed leaf-thatched hut. The latter might sound attractive, but the overwhelming presence of cockroaches and ants made it less appropriate until a major spring-clean had been performed. There were, of course, no toilets nor any running water. Water had to be fetched from afar.

The people had been waiting for hours in the centres where the dispensary calls women shivering with fever, men with huge tropical ulcers, children with dysentery and malaria, all of them suffering from malnutrition and anaemia. In addition there was always a chapter of accidents. Someone had swallowed poison and lay unconscious. A child had fallen into the fire. The witch doctor had smeared paint on the wounds and it took Eva nearly two hours to clean that off and give antibiotics. A lad had fallen on broken glass and was badly cut, requiring many stitches. A man had been knocked down by a car and carried in seriously injured. He must be given first aid, then taken to hospital.

The regular visitors to the dispensary included expectant mothers in great numbers, and hundreds of mothers with young babies. The average number of patients treated daily was around one hundred and fifty. For some years Eva den Hartog could not take any annual holiday because there was no one to replace her. Her health suffered in the long run, but she made time each day for prayer and drawing strength from God. Even with a hectic programme she wrote, 'I need the moments with God. I need to be in His presence. In moments of prayer the Holy Spirit comes to me, giving me strength to do His work.'

After the 1964 war, lightly-wounded soldiers were sent for treatment to the Salvation Army clinic which had been erected in Masina, laying an extra duty on the over-burdened small staff of nurses. Some of these soldiers were just boys of fifteen and sixteen. White people were so hated at that time in the former Congo, that dislike and contempt could be read on the soldiers' faces even while white hands were tending their wounds. It was not an easy situation. Problems increased. Food was very scarce and political chaos caused much sporadic fighting. It was dangerous to go out at night.

The year 1967 brought a much-needed homeland furlough with rest and medical treatment for the tired nursing sister. But Eva was not the resting sort! She managed to visit the United States, Canada and Denmark, leading meetings, giving interviews on television and radio, and of course the Netherlands laid its own claim on her time and she became *news*. Queen Juliana awarded Eva den Hartog the high honour of Knight of the Oranje Nassau 'for devotion and efficiency in the execution of her lofty task in Congo'.

It was a heavily-laden Eva who returned to Zaïre in 1968. She had with her two ambulances which had been donated, and also many boxes of medical equipment and medicines. Two years more she was able to devote to her clinics; then health difficulties made a return to Europe desirable.

The next trouble-spot for Major Eva den Hartog was Calcutta in 1971 where streams of refugees and destitute families were swelling the seething mass of humanity in and around that city. Eva was becoming an expert in such situations, and she was later sent to help the Netherlands Red Cross in Bangladesh for three months. Having seen the need on the spot, she returned to her homeland to organise a Salvation Army social-medical team, which started its ministry in Bangladesh in 1972, with Dacca as its headquarters.

One of the centres chosen for involvement was Faridpur, a town of thirty thousand inhabitants. There was a small hospital in very bad condition. With only eighty beds, it had more than a hundred patients, many of them lying in the grounds, hungry, untended, some dying. Everywhere there was a terrible smell. The Army medical team was asked to help train the staff.

The deputy commissioner asked the team to interest itself in a newly opened children's home. Two hundred and fifty children arrived the first week, and a similar number was on its way. Food was already problematic. The kitchen was just a small shed. There were no beds; the children were sleeping on the floor.

Weekly clinics were started and hundreds were treated. All were hungry — mothers holding up tiny babies like skeletons and old people, too weak to walk, being helped along. Malnutrition and anaemia were so advanced in many cases that there was little hope of averting death. In addition, there were the usual dysentery, skin diseases, ulcers and sores.

Six months later, in November 1972, the report strikes a brighter note. Conditions of the villagers were improving. The children of the two orphanages had been vaccinated against polio, and primary schools were the next on the list. Patients were still attending the clinics from as far as thirty and forty miles away. They slept out all night to be sure of attention next morning. As the nights are quite cold, the team distributed blankets donated by the Mennonite Central Committee.

The Army team is not only interested in giving medical help. There is also an experimental agricultural plot where farmers can come to observe and learn. Because of the hot climate everything grows quickly and with seeds and material given by the Southern Baptist Mission there can be a succession of fresh vegetables both for consumption and demonstration.

For the moment Major Eva den Hartog is still hard at work in Bangladesh, but where God's hand will next lead her, she cannot see. She is content to have it so, for she is a fully-committed servant of God. If officership in The Salvation Army has thrown her into many dangerous situations, it has given her a sense of fulfilment and purpose for her life.

CHAPTER TEN

Writers Plus

THE Salvation Army has been rich through the years in its
women writers, but the doyenne of them all is Commissioner
Catherine Bramwell-Booth, now in her nineties. The two extensive biographies which she has produced, one of her father,
Bramwell Booth,* and the other of her grandmother, *Catherine
Booth: The Story of her Loves*,† are monuments to her facility
of expression, and give authentic glimpses into the thought-
and-action world of the Army's founders.

Commissioner Catherine lives with two sisters in a sprawling
house and garden near Reading, with enough Army atmosphere
around her to keep alive memories of feet marching and flags
flying to the roll of drums and martial music. Army symbols
give a military impression to one part of the long lounge. The
'Blood-and-Fire' flag — its blue-red-yellow folds neatly
draped — rests in the corner. A large drum adorned with the
Army crest stands beside it. But the Commissioner does not
live in the past. Her alert mind follows the topics of the day. In
1971 she became a Commander of the British Empire.

In advanced age Catherine Bramwell-Booth is still soldier-
straight and at her ease on a platform. Her public speaking has
an unforgettable quality about it and big occasions do not intimi-

* Rich and Cowan.

† Hodder and Stoughton.

date her. She has preached in Bergen Cathedral, Norway, and St. Giles, Edinburgh. During her years as the international secretary for Europe she preached in Prague, Helsinki and St. Petersburg (now Leningrad), but in the latter city it was behind closed shutters and drawn curtains. In council deliberations she revealed a crystal-clear and penetrating mind. She could see right to the kernel of a problem and grasped details with amazing insight.

In her earlier service she was engaged in training women cadets, and those young women treasure the little book she wrote specially for them, *Messages to the Messengers*. In it she writes simply, straight from a warm and understanding heart. Another of her productions is the small book of verse published in 1930, entitled *A Few Lines*. Here the intense, mystic side of her nature is revealed, with a great love for the countryside.

Commissioner Catherine's leadership qualities were evident from the beginning but they were particularly useful in the training of cadets. She not only told cadets how things should be done; she also showed them. There was the day of the Silvertown disaster when an East End munitions factory exploded near by, killing sixty and injuring four hundred. Catherine summoned the Army cadets, packed baskets with food and milk and set out. Flames lit up the whole sky. The area was barricaded off and guarded by police who would allow no one in. Catherine marched her cadets right up to the barriers and told the police, 'We're going in!' and in they went to give succour and comfort.

In July 1972 Commissioner Bramwell-Booth spoke in a Home League Rally at Wembley Pool to nine thousand women, the Duchess of Kent being present. The audience was enthusiastic in its response to the Commissioner's forthright, challenging address. Her delightful humour and her momentary demonstration of operatic singing were received with tumultuous applause. One of her joking remarks was, 'Most old people are grandmas. I'm not. I must have missed the boat somewhere!' If she did, that was surely the only boat she has ever missed in her long life!

*　　*　　*

One of Denmark's leading women officers, Lt.-Colonel Ketty Røper, spent thirty-three years on editorial work. She is one of those people who can do nothing by half measures. At the time of her conversion she worked in a lawyer's office in Copenhagen. One Sunday evening a few months later she enrolled as a Salvation Army soldier in full uniform. The next morning she arrived at work in her uniform and sat down at her desk. The lawyer eyed her for a few moments, then asked, 'Is it really necessary that you wear that uniform to the office?' Ketty nodded, wondering how matters would go. Fortunately for her the lawyer had a well developed sense of humour, for he just laughed and said, 'Then I shall be the only lawyer in the city with a uniformed secretary!'

A young couple came in one day seeking a divorce and Ketty received them and heard their story. Full of new born zeal for God's cause she reasoned with them, finally prayed with them and sent them home reconciled. Her employer stated that she was bad for his business, but he said it with a twinkle in his eye. When Ketty announced that she would be leaving him to start service with The Salvation Army he protested, saying that she would make a good solicitor and that he would himself pay for her studies. Ketty, however, was fully intent on following the call she had received from God. She was by then a deep-dyed salvationist, affirming that her very blood was striped yellow, red and blue!

After training as an officer in Copenhagen she was appointed to evangelical work in the provinces. It was a new world for the girl from the lawyer's office, but her field experience was short-lived, for she was soon drafted into the editorial office at head-quarters.

In 1948 Ketty was invited to the re-opening of Hope Town Women's Hostel in London, where many celebrities were present. It was a grand occasion but her piquant sense of curiosity made her want to know the difference between being an honoured guest and being an inmate. Having tried the one she decided to try the other.

Late next night she arrived at the hostel incognito. Frowsy hair, torn and soiled clothes, were only part of the disguise. She had also blacked over a few of her teeth. She knocked . . . and knocked . . . but nothing happened. The road was empty at that time of night, but in a house farther down a man opened a bedroom window and bawled, 'Ye'll not get in there ternight. They're full up and the door's locked. Buzz off!'

Even if 'buzz off' was beyond Ketty's academic knowledge of English, she grasped the message conveyed by the angry voice and waving arm. As she slunk down the road, keeping well to the shadows, she met a policeman. To him she confided that she had been turned out by the folk she lived with after a quarrel and had nowhere to go for the night. He took her to the police-station.

He was a friendly bobby, very interested in the strange woman he had picked up, but he didn't seem to believe her story. Again and again he asked, 'Why are you here? Who are you? Tell me the truth.' To all of which Ketty could answer that her home was in another land and she wanted a bed for the night.

He made her a cup of cocoa. When it came to two a.m. Ketty

decided the moment had come to reveal the truth. The immediacy with which he believed her rather shook her faith in her disguise! She told him that she was a Salvation Army editor in Denmark, and she wanted to write a first-hand account of a night at Hope Town for her paper. He thought it would have been a fine idea if only she had tried it out earlier in the evening. There being no other car available, he got out the Black Maria and trundled the would-be vagrant across London to her temporary billet.

A couple of days later she rang at the door of Hope Town early in the evening, clad in the same shoddy clothes as before, teeth newly blacked over. This time the door was opened by a tiny gnome of an officer, very sweet and helpful. Ketty's heart nearly missed a beat. It was the very major she had sat next to at the opening reception. But her disguise held its secret. The newcomer was allotted a bed in a room for twelve and a girl was asked to take her down to the dining-room for tea and sandwiches. The rest of the evening Ketty spent with the other 'ladies', as they were generously called, in the sitting-room.

Ten o'clock was bedtime and everyone trundled off to the dormitories, but the lively chatter continued long after the ladies had kissed each other goodnight and climbed into their clean but hard beds.

Ketty lay awake for a very long time with her eleven companions very near, hearing their muttered comments, their chirpy happiness at having a bed to creep into, and finally their snores. Friends asked her afterwards if she wasn't afraid to sleep in a dormitory with so many unknown women from the streets of London. Yes, she had been afraid, she confessed, but not in the sense they meant: not of smells or dirt or a possible straying flea. What she had dreaded was to find that the loving care of the officers in charge would be too limited, too fragile, to stretch out to each woman in the crowd; that in the pressure of their tasks they would reveal irritability or indifference. Her fears were groundless. She was received kindly and the snatches of conversation from bed to bed at night — none realising that a spy was present — were about the kindness of the staff, the matron being named with real affection.

At eight o'clock next morning, Sunday, the dormitory door opened and a cheerful voice wished them all 'Good morning and a pleasant day', adding that breakfast could be eaten up to nine o'clock but that any lady who wished might remain in bed until ten. The almost sleepless hours that Ketty had spent in Hope Town were enough for her. She had found out what she had come to discover. Up and dressed, she was seen to the door by a friendly captain who wished her God's blessing.

Ketty Røper's natural aptitude for literary expression was polished and perfected over the years until she became a master of words. To her was given the task of writing the history of The Salvation Army in Denmark, to commemorate its seventy-fifth anniversary in 1962. It is a unique Army history, being well-spiced with humour and challenge, and enlivened by a couple of dozen cartoons as well as the usual photographs. Lt.-Colonel Ketty Røper admits with cheerful frankness to having dropped a spark here and there in the gunpowder in the hope that it might say *bang* in the right place.

*   *   *

Another author of Salvation Army history is the indefatigable writer Sallie Chesham of the United States. Sparks fly when she takes a pen into her hand, her natural bent sharpened by studies in journalism at Northwestern University. Mrs. Colonel Sallie Chesham is now serving with her husband in New York, her own interests being special assignments in writing and public speaking.

She wrote *Born to Battle*,* the Army history with a foreword by General Dwight D. Eisenhower, which gives a swiftly-moving kaleidoscopic account of the Army's phenomenal growth in the States.

Sallie Chesham is a career writer who has produced more than four hundred feature-articles, stories, booklets, plays and pageants. She is included in *Who's Who in Women of the World* and *International Biography of Women*, is a member of the Society of Midland Authors and an honorary member of the London Women's Press Club. Of her three books of poetry, *Walking with the Wind*† won her the Chicago Poetry Award for 1970. Her verses reveal a profound spiritual awareness of God and His Spirit. She writes in modern idiom, her verses having a swing and a rhythm that make them instantly appealing, even compelling. Her own comment is, 'If the poems have any importance, it must be that they express my yearning after God and my near ecstasy in sometimes actually touching the hem of His glorious garment. At those times there is a strange exhilaration of peace combined with power.'

Sallie has a lot of energy in her small frame. While based in Chicago she personally organised and founded The Old Hat, a coffee house in a five-roomed store front. It was situated in a poor settlement area of the inner city, where fifteen thousand black families lived within an area of two blocks. She felt deeply about the drop-outs from school, runaways from home, drug-addicts and the destitute, and when that happens she becomes a crusader with fire and fury for anything and anyone in her path. As a certified social worker she is well equipped

---

* Rand McNally and Co.
† Word Publishers.

with a background knowledge of theory, but only her personal courage and her staunch faith in the presence of Christ enable her to tackle the violent, unpredictable gangs of outcasts. The Old Hat programme includes a drop-in centre for teenagers, many of whom are gang members; children's and women's work; emergency aid to families; and correctional institution work, all in an attempt to communicate Christ on the streets of Chicago's near-north side.

Sallie Chesham's book *Trouble doesn't happen Next Tuesday** tells the story of her involvement with a coloured youth gang. It was no easy task. It required a tremendous degree of faith and fortitude, of persistent friendliness and un-shockability, and often heroism. She writes, 'My work has been strange and hazardous. It is based on the premise that if you want to do something constructive about trouble, you've got to go where it is. Our boys have been beaten, maimed, shot stabbed and killed; sometimes . . . have done the same. At a time when the police take in gang boys for walking two abreast on the street, we can still have a party for one hundred and fifty without mishap. Maybe it's even more difficult to roam the concrete slab called North Avenue than the rippling waves of Lake Galilee, but we know a winner who both walks and talks on our street . . . Christ is the Head of the Old Hat family. We figure if we never quit we can't lose. We march on.'

A probation officer asked Sallie if she did not feel afraid to work amid such dangers. Her answer was typical, 'I realise I may be expendable, but God put me here and I have faith. Isn't that what being a Christian means — being expendable?'

Sallie Chesham is a third-generation salvationist and has been an officer since 1940. Indefatigable in her many-sided ministry, she has time for her husband and two children, al-

* Word Publishers.

though she readily admits that it is easier now when the children are grown-up and have left home. What new crusade she may attempt in future days is unknown, but one thing is sure: if Sallie Chesham takes it up, it will succeed.

* * *

Captain Majken Johansson of Sweden has published six books of verse and her story is quite unusual. An unhappy child, brought up by a harsh foster-mother bordering on insanity, Majken developed into a very disharmonious young woman. There was nothing wrong with her intellect, though. While a student at Lund University she contributed an article to the press entitled 'God, Morals and Conscience', in which she proved to her own satisfaction that one of the three existed outside the realm of imagination. She started a students' literary club, all of them free-thinkers, atheists, and hard-hitting realists. Her hyper-modernistic verse began to appear in the press and in 1952 her first book of poems was published. The reviewers used such terms as 'pungent and impudent', 'neck-breaking irony'.

At the age of twenty-three, her Master of Science degree assured, Majken moved north to Stockholm, already a chain-smoker and in the grip of severe alcoholism. In her sober moments she wrote verse and did translations to bring in some money. In 1956 her second book of poetry was published. Meanwhile she sank deeper into the morass of drink, knowing the horror of *delirium tremens* and the insecurity of a vagrants's life.

At last in her despair she searched through a telephone directory for the word 'alcohol' and found the address of an advice bureau. There a friendly and understanding doctor started her on a course of treatment which included psychoanalysis. For two years she continued her sessions on the analyst's couch.

A friend she loved deeply lay dying, and some irreconcilable instinct within caused her to throw herself on her knees in her Stockholm flat and pray to the God whose existence she denied. The friend died, but Majken continued to pray, this time for herself.

Early in 1958, as she walked the city streets, she saw a man standing in the trampled snow giving out what looked like long sweets in coloured cellophane paper. She accepted one, opened it, and found a printed paper from an address in the United States. There were two squares to mark with an X: 'Do you believe in Jesus Christ?' and 'Do you want to know about Jesus Christ?' With a kind of daring, Majken put an X in the first square, added her address and posted the paper, then forgot all about it.

Once when visiting her analyst she asked him, 'Where should one go if one wants to become a real Christian?' Majken Johanssen was tired of being alone, tired of her solitary quest after God, her aimless attendance at one church after another in search of a spiritual home. 'Well,' said the doctor thoughtfully, 'you could go to The Salvation Army. They have plenty of songs and music.'

Majken was twenty-eight, but she had never met the Army. She went to a near-by hall, sitting as close to the exit as possible in case she wanted to beat a hasty retreat. The meeting was led by a group of young women cadets. Majken was intrigued by the way they marched in to joyous singing and rhythmic hand-clapping. She listened critically, yet fascinated by their testimonies.

In the next meeting she attended, on the Sunday night, emotion conquered her and she began to cry. Someone slipped into the seat beside her and asked whether she wanted to go forward to the Penitent Form. No! She was not prepared for that. At the close of the meeting a woman officer spoke to her and this time Majken accepted her invitation to go forward in the almost empty hall to kneel at the Form and pray.

As she went home that evening, Majken's heart was filled with contradictory sentiments: joy that she had taken a decisive step; hatred of herself for having done so. Her mind a battle-field of opposing elements, she was conscious of one dominant desire: to smoke. Salvationists didn't smoke. Well, she did. And would! She lit a cigarette and puffed aggressively.

Next morning when she said her prayers Majken noticed with astonishment that the atmosphere of her room was charged with some sort of spiritual power, which enveloped her, filling her with joy. Then the postman came with a small packet from America, a pocket-sized copy of St. John's gospel from the American Bible Union. Majken sat down to read. While at university she had more than once decided to read the Bible, not from religious conviction or desire, but simply for general knowledge. Each time she had been bogged down in the swamps of genealogical lists in Genesis, and got no further. St. John's gospel was different and, of course, Majken was now different, too. With joy and tears she read it right through. 'Behold the Lamb of God which taketh away the sin of the world.' It had happened to her, Majken Johansson. The faltering prayer she had sent up to God from the Army's Penitent Form hadn't just vanished into thin air. Here was the reply. Personally and intensely, she met Jesus Christ as her Saviour, there in her own room. The pocket gospel which had taken three months to reach her arrived at the very moment she needed it.

Her first impulse was to conquer cigarette smoking. There was an anti-smoking clinic within cycling distance and there she was given advice, tablets and injections. She noticed with an ironical smile that never before had cigarette advertisements appeared so alluring or tobacconists so numerous. With the first money saved from smoking she bought herself a wooden crucifix carved in Oberammergau. Hanging on her wall, it gave immense strength to her resolution.

A few days later she stood on the pavement watching an Army procession march by to spirited music. Swinging along with the rest was the officer who had prayed with Majken at the Penitent Form. The salvationist left the march, took Majken's arm, and with a smile led her into the procession, the only one in civilian clothes among all the uniforms. In an instant there flashed through Majken's brain all the writers, poets, and business folk and others who might recognise her, but then the joy of belonging to the marching soldiers of God outweighed her fears.

The march halted at the market place for an open-air meeting. To Majken's horror she saw in the crowd a couple of old cronies from her drinking days. When the service was over the two shot over to her, and she steeled herself against the expected taunts. Instead there were friendly smiles and her erstwhile pals said, 'You've got to come home with us and tell us what's happened.' So over a cup of coffee Majken gave her first testimony: 'I believe in God and I'm saved.'

The new convert soon advanced to the recruit stage and was permitted to wear on her coat the army's red-yellow-blue tricolour ribbon. To make sure that all her coats and jackets should bear witness to her new allegiance, she bought yards of the ribbon, quite enough to decorate a dozen recruits. Next day her telephone rang. A publisher, unknown to her by name, had seen her in a bookshop with a narrow ribbon in her lapel. What did it mean? 'Oh,' replied Majken happily, 'it means that I've joined The Salvation Army.' Two days later newspapers bore the striking notice MAJKEN JOHANSSON HAS JOINED THE SALVATION ARMY! There was no longer need for any recruit ribbon. All the world now knew. Majken's bridges were burned behind her.

Three months later she was enrolled as a salvation soldier in full uniform. She knew that some form of service was now expected of her. The choice was not easy, but she finally decided to sell the *War Cry* to other homes in the block of flats where she lived. The following year she was a cadet in the Stockholm Training College and on being commissioned an officer she was appointed to editorial work at headquarters.

A film version of Majken Johansson's life story has been produced for churches in Sweden, and she is often quoted in the press and interviewed on radio and television. She receives many invitations to tell of her conversion and in a simple artless way she plays her guitar and sings salvation songs. The one-time atheist, chain-smoker and alcoholic is now a Salvation Army captain, dedicated to win others for God.

CHAPTER ELEVEN

With Faith and Floorcloth

IN 1928 a Fleet Street journalist, Hugh Redwood, 'discovered' the Army's slum sisters in Westminster where the Thames had overflowed its banks. Amid the squelchy slime of the flooded area Mr. Redwood wrote his greatest news story, followed by the book *God in the Slums*.* But the slum sisters had already been at their compassionate cleaning-up campaign with faith and floorcloth for forty years!

It began in 1884 with the euphonious name of the Cellar, Gutter and Garret Brigade. These haunts were the customary spheres of action for young officers and cadets, clad for their new role with praiseworthy modesty. Even a handkerchief was taboo; it might be taken to indicate classiness. Dressed in cotton frocks, aprons and shawls, hard black straw boaters adorned with a simple Army crest on their heads, they carried the tools of their trade: pail, broom, floorcloth and a small first-aid kit. They scrubbed floors, cleaned verminous bodies, lit fires in cold rooms and fed and washed neglected children. They did it with a smile and a 'God bless you'. Before leaving they prayed if they were allowed to do so.

Slum people of the old days were not always happy at being cleaned up. It made them feel a little like shorn lambs. They

* Hodder and Stoughton.

would no doubt have subscribed to the humorous dictum, 'A little dirt makes for cosiness; a lot, for warmth.' But the slum sisters were stern about cleanliness and were energetic in their war against filth and lice. 'Cleanliness is next to godliness' could have been emblazoned on their banner. They lived in the slums, usually in one small room in a tenement. One young officer was challenged by a frowsy woman, who declared vehemently that it was all right to be happy and religious when one had whole boots on one's feet, but not when they were patched and holey. Sitting down on the doorstep the lieutenant quickly pulled off her boots, handing them to the astonished and delighted woman. The poor lieutenant found she had made a bad exchange, for she had to tie the acquired footgear on with lengths of string and even then they flopped about. But she felt that she had proved her point, and was still rejoicing in the Lord. One slum sister was greatly concerned about an old couple who had only wooden boxes to sit on in their one room. She hunted around and at last found a cheap second-hand armchair. With a colleague's help she got it up the narrow stairs to the attic room where the old people lived. What a rapturous reception awaited them! A few days later she returned, expecting to find the frail old lady at ease in the chair, but no, it was the husband who was enthroned there, while his wife leaned against the wall, gazing at her partner in his glory. But the chair had been bought for *her*, the lieutenant explained, for she was the more frail. 'Oh, missy, he's only takin' 'is turn. We sits in it by turns and praise be it's nearly me own turn now!'

Soon slum posts were established with a small meeting-hall attached, where officers could hold gatherings with those they visited during the day. It was a pale shadow of the future community centres, but it was a gesture that was appreciated by slum-dwellers. Slum work expanded all over Great Britain and in other lands where the Army had its operations. In 1930 the Goodwill League was started, with Hugh Redwood as its first president, to enlist the active interest of people from all walks of life who could give spare-time service to the poor under the motto 'Such as I have, give I'.

With the abolition of slums and the word 'slum', the Army's slum posts were re-christened Goodwill Centres. There are now thirty-one of them throughout Britain.

A small boy, trying to spell out the red lettering across one captain's apron, managed to get it right. 'G-o-o-d-w-i-l-l. But what does it mean, Captain?' 'What do you think?' she asked. He considered for a moment and the said, 'Well, you're good and you're willin', ain't you?' It was a good definition.

Goodwill officers will tell you that the welfare is not a generous panacea for all life's ills. There are still lonely, broken-hearted and desperate people, families facing sudden emergencies, parents almost crazed with anxiety about their children. These people need someone to talk to who is kind and understanding, and who will pray to God for them and with them: the Goodwill officer. She is never unemployed or on strike. The hours of her day are filled to the limit.

Some officers were asked to visit a lady doctor, long ago struck from the register because of her alcoholism, and now with drug addiction as an added problem. She had refused a home help, but the Army lassies managed to win her friendship and were admitted. Many things, such as blankets, rugs and woollies, were full of moths. Packets of cake and biscuits were mouldy. The house was unheated, without any gas or electricity supply, cut off because the doctor had not paid the bills.

What a task faced the officer! Sorting, burning, throwing out and clearing up took a whole fortnight before the operation was concluded. The old lady caught the frenzy of effort and herself polished the old black stove in the kitchen. One day as she sat in the easy chair in her living-room she exclaimed with delight, 'Why, Captain, I can see the pattern on the lino! It's nothing short of a miracle.' Years of grime had been scrubbed away and the roses were now visible. It is not so easy, though, to remove the effect of evil on the old lady. She comes to the meetings, and the officers were thrilled to hear her say, 'Please go on praying for me.' Who knows, perhaps a miracle will occur in her life too, by God's grace.

Brigadier Martha Field of the Nottingham Goodwill Centre knew all there was to know of the seamy side of life. She herself was well known to the police, but certainly not as a trouble-maker. She was the policeman's ally. When he needed her in the night he flashed his strong torch on to the ceiling in her bedroom. The light woke her and soon she was dressed and ready to receive him. Sometimes he brought a runaway girl found on the street, or a mother and children afraid to go home because father was fighting-drunk.

Another night a call might come to pray with a man dying in a nearby lodging-house. He had asked for the 'Captain', re-membering that she had a kind word for him in the street one day. Sometimes a neighbour battered at the door in panic to say that there was a street fight and someone would be killed if the Army didn't intervene. Life has certainly never proved monotonous for Martha Field. Fortunately she is well endowed with courage and determination, despite her slight build.

One night the constable's flashing light woke her to receive a seventeen-year-old mother with her tiny baby. Her parents had cast her off and from one lodging to another Lottie had been moved on, everyone complaining of the baby's constant wail-ing. The little mite was obviously underfed and suffering. The policeman had found Lottie crouched in the shelter of a house wall, cold and soaked with rain, helplessly clutching the crying child.

A warm bath and food for both Lottie and her baby worked wonders but the shock of seeing the neglected little one followed. When its soaked and soiled nappy was removed, parts of the inflamed skin came with it, leaving raw flesh exposed. No wonder the child had cried so incessantly. Softly massaged with oil and cosily wrapped, the infant dropped off into a deep sleep. Part of Martha's job was to teach Lottie how to look after her baby and to find a situation where she could have the child with her.

Martha Field was not only well known among the women of the district; she was also popular among the old men in the lodging-houses. When they were ill they sent her a message asking for a visit. Not easily shocked, Martha nevertheless blinked her eyes occasionally at the state of extreme undress in which these gentlemen lodgers received her. From a dirty blanket an emaciated hand like a bird's claw would clutch at the cup which she held out. One old man had lain unattended so long on his bed that he had to be prised up from the soiled and caked bedding, losing patches of his skin in the process. One needs a strong sense of vocation to deal with such situations without faltering.

Another man asked a special favour of the Brigadier. Would she fetch his new teeth that he had been measured for because the doctor had told him he had only one month to live. Martha strongly doubted that any doctor would give such a definite forecast of death, so she remarked jokingly, 'If you've got a month to live, you won't need your new teeth!' 'But I will,' retorted the man, 'for they say there's going to be weeping and gnashing of teeth and I want to have some teeth to gnash!' The old man got his teeth but he is still very much alive!

In the small meetings which Brigadier Field conducted, she was always conscious of being the pastor, not only a social worker. Her heart yearned over the seekers with true motherly care. One night a prostitute made a decision for Christ, to Martha's great joy. In her elation she promised God, 'I'll do anything to keep her yours, Lord, *anything*!' She little knew at that time just what that word would embrace.

The new convert fell ill with abdominal cancer. The two Goodwill officers nursed her, taking a half-night of sleep alternately. The stench became so bad that they had to use face masks dipped in strong disinfectant, so powerful that it blistered their mouths. When the end neared the smell was so foul that a welfare officer and a neighbour who had called to offer help simply fainted in the passage. Martha Field offered a prayer to God for help, then went in to wash the body and prepare it for burial. Her convert had died in the faith.

One group of the community that the Goodwill officers visit regularly is that of prisoners' wives. They are sometimes much more to be pitied than their erring husbands. Martha saw the bitter irony of the situation when she visited a mother with seven children in bed with measles. The room was squalid, cold and smelly with enclosed air. There was very little food and no money to buy more. The mother had just received a letter from the husband in prison. 'I'm thinking of you, darling. The radio is just now playing "Love's old sweet song".'

One task that Martha Field has always enjoyed is cleaning up old folks, not because it is a pleasant job but because they look so lovely afterwards. She has to coax them first, promising to use a special shampoo or wonder-soap or scented talcum powder. It is quite a feat of agility and physical endurance to get them in and out of the bath without mishap and with as little grumbling as possible. Then fresh clothes and combed hair, and a slow delight spreads over the wrinkled faces. It's good to be clean! And finally, a cup of tea and a nap.

In 1969 Brigadier Martha Field married and is now, in retirement, Mrs. Lt.-Colonel Wilfrid Osborne.

* * *

Kilburn Goodwill Centre in North London is a constant hive of activity. Ann Pollard is an experienced Goodwill officer who has seen service in England, Scotland and Wales. With her helpers she meets many needs in the community, but they are in desperate need of larger accommodation. To cook a nourishing hot meal twice weekly and then to be able to seat only eighty guests at the Centre, leaves many out. One old man, when told that his name would be put on the waiting-list, asked pathetically, 'Do you think enough people will have died for me to come to the Christmas dinner?'

Handicapped people enjoy a meal once a week at a time reserved specially for them. The Over-Sixty club numbers a hundred, and there is even an Over-Eighty group which sings together. For many people of the district the Goodwill Centre is the focal point of their lives.

To the loneliness of old age has been added another poignant fear — that of being assaulted, either in the street or while alone at home. The Goodwill officer must be a frequent visitor, easily available when panic threatens, and leaving comfort and courage behind her.

To move from a squalid downstairs room to a top flat in a high building where light and air circulate might seem a heaven-sent solution to an old lady. But for Mrs. S. the utopia did not last long, for she had not reckoned with the lift. She had been glad there was a lift. Her bad legs would not have managed the long flights of stone stairs. But that the plaguey thing should make so much noise and clatter she had not envisaged. Clash, bang, thump, rattle ... From four a.m. until well after midnight the metallic monster chanted its hellish cacophony. Mrs. S. told herself she would get used to it. She lay with a pillow over her ear, tense and nervous. Sleep would not come. The grinding of the machinery continued in her head even when all was silent around her.

She had welcomed the light and air, talking cheerfully of being nearer heaven, but now she seemed very far from earth and neighbours. She began to get jittery, a bag of nerves, more and more isolated. One night brought her a real fright. She woke to find she had walked in her sleep out on to the small balcony. One foot was over the metal rail; its coldness had wakened her. Shaking with terror and chilled to the bone she crept back into her room. Packing the furniture against the balcony door, she curled up in an armchair and pleaded with God to help and succour her.

The solution when it came was two-fold. Brigadier Pollard invited her to the Goodwill centre where she met other elderly people. The officers took an interest in her and visited her. A lady doctor, realising the cause of Mrs. S.'s nerves, recommended that another flat should be found for her. Mrs. S. agreed to move but was adamant on one point. She would not go outside the district. She must be near the Goodwill Centre!

That story illustrates the isolation of old people but there is also the loneliness of the disturbed teenager.

One evening while on her rounds the Goodwill officer heard crying coming from a basement. Going down the steps to investigate, she found two teenage sisters huddled together to keep warm, very hungry, and terrified of the rats which were running around the floor. They explained that after their mother's death their father had attempted to assault them sexually, so they had run away. The officer took them home, gave them a hot meal, a bath, clean clothes and a bed. Employment was found for them in a holiday home at the seaside, and there they felt safe and settled down happily.

*   *   *

The name Faith Cottage conjures up a rural setting, with an old-fashioned garden and roses round the door, but this Faith Cottage lay close to King's Cross station, a tiny house squeezed in among not-too-clean neighbours, with the hum of traffic ever present and a strong London smell as its permanent atmosphere. And yet it was an ideal place for Brigadier Mary Scott to live, not for her own sake, but for those she could help.

For one thing, it was close to a big railway terminus, and Mary Scott and other social workers know that a railway station is the scene of many incipient tragedies. Foolish girls who leave home to take a train to London, believing that an exciting life with many thrilling adventures awaits them; runaways who in a fit of anger or opposition decide to show mum and dad that they are grown-up and can manage their own lives; the distressed traveller whose friends do not meet her as arranged, all these and many more are vulnerable to the men who wait and watch, ready to pounce.

Mary Scott is not the hefty police-woman type. Her voice is quiet, her eyes steady rather than penetrating, and her smile is kindly. Girls and women feel that they can trust her and the uniform she wears, so they are not afraid when she accosts them in the street. She is on the look-out for those who need a bed for the night or motherly counsel. Sometimes the police would bring strangers to her door but Faith Cottage had not much to offer in the way of accommodation. There was only one small single room, with a possibility of using a divan as a second bed. So Faith Cottage had to go, and for two years there was a gap where it had stood. Now that gap had been filled by Faith House, a larger structure with four beds. Sometimes Mary slept on cushions on the floor to leave her own bed for a fifth person.

Years on salvationist midnight patrol service in London gave Mary Scott valid experience plus a certain intuition in sizing up a situation. But she has not spent all her life in the metropolis. Born in a Cumberland village, the middle child of five, she attended school until the age of fourteen. She had been confirmed in the Church of England, but interest in The Salvation Army was aroused and in 1941 she became a cadet in the London Training College. Appointed to do social work, she served in several institutions and was then chosen as midnight patrol and prison officer, particularly for women and girls caught up in the vice trade in London.

By visiting women in prison Mary won their confidence and on their release she was able to help them to a new way of life. Not all result in success stories, but that is hardly to be expected with the kind of material she has worked with. What gave her particular joy was to be able to allay the fears of parents by tracing their errant daughters and persuading them to return home before their life was too deeply enmeshed in vice.

One Irish girl was sent to Faith House by the police. Her boyfriend had brought her over, promising marriage, as he knew she was pregnant by him. However, when he found out that she could neither cook nor housekeep, he began to knock her about. Bruised and frightened, she appealed to the police who sent her to Mary Scott. The boy found out where she was and continued to pester her. One day he forced his way into Faith House and dragged her screaming into the street. Rescued by the police, she was returned to the care of Brigadier Scott. The boy was charged by the police, but the pregnant girl felt she would be safer in her homeland and so returned to Ireland. But she still writes to Mary Scott.

Not only young girls find their way to Faith House. There was Mrs. T., for instance, seventy-seven years old, who arrived tottery and dishevelled and very vague in speech and manner. When her story was pieced together, Brigadier Scott found that she had emigrated to Australia when young and married there. When her husband died she seemed to lose her grip on life, shutting herself away in the house and becoming suspicious of the neighbours. They retaliated by leaving her alone. She was taken ill and was eventually moved to hospital. In answer to all questions she would only say that she had relatives in England; so when she was better she was put on a plane and sent 'home'.

Mrs. T. had been away from England for fifty years, and the only address she had was that of a niece. But the niece was married and lived in a caravan. There was hardly room for one more, and that a complete stranger. Old Mrs. T. took to wandering and was picked up many times by the police. One day she decided on a trip to London and simply walked out and took a train. On arrival, dazed and tired, she was noticed by the police who took her to Faith House. It was not easy to find the right solution to her problem but finally Brigadier Scott was able to trace some relatives in the north of England who were willing to take the old lady. Mrs. T. was of very independent character and on the day of departure she insisted on paying her own fare, for which she took out two half-crowns. When told that the ticket would cost ten times that much, she was aghast. 'Why couldn't they leave England as it was before?' she asked. A very good question!

One evening a woman asked for accommodation at Faith House but unfortunately there was none available, so she was recommended to try another address. A few minutes later she knocked again but this time forced her way in and began beating the officer on the head. The pet poodle seized the woman's skirt in its teeth and as she turned to kick the dog, she was hustled over the threshold. With lightning quickness she seized a milk-bottle standing on the step and lunged at the officer, who ducked automatically. The bottle smashed through the glass panel with a frightful noise. Army officers reckon it to be part of their job to be prepared for such attacks, but fortunately they do not come often. This particular woman proved to be a meths drinker, given to sudden outbursts of violence.

Brigadier Mary Scott has now begun her retirement. Her life has been full of adventure, but much that has happened must be kept by her in confidence. To God she can speak about the needs of her friends, but her lips must be sealed to others.

*   *   *

Another Goodwill officer, Alice Sigsworth, was led by circumstances to serve the deaf whom she found in great numbers in London. She gave herself so energetically and wholeheartedly to this task that the Sigsworth Hall at Bethnal Green was named after her. Alice was active, boisterous, outgoing, her contagious laugh and Yorkshire accent winning her friends at short notice. She was generous to a fault: she gave away not only her own shoes and clothes, but also those of her assistant.

Starting her Army career as a lieutenant at the Ann Fowler Home in Liverpool, Alice was sent to the market with some empty sacks to ask for gifts of fish. To make a good impression she put on her new uniform. The fishmongers knew the Army and came with hands full of cods' heads, haddock, mackerel, sprats and herrings, pushing the slippery, strong-smelling fish into her sacks. All Alice did was to smile and nod her thanks.

The sacks were now smelly and wet, and too heavy to carry. Alice waited for a tram, then another and another . . . No conductor would allow her plus her sacks on his tram! She had to walk, half dragging the sacks after her, her new coat well covered with scales and slime and smelling to highest heaven. Her only consolation was to see — later in the day — the folk of the Home enjoying their dinner of fish. She learnt not to use her parade uniform for market-day.

Captain Sigsworth was later appointed to Bethnal Green, where she was to spend twenty-one years. She was fortunate in having Eleanor Gebbie as her assistant. When Eleanor arrived, the captain received her with the typical words, 'Hullo, luv. Why, you're nowt but a kid!' From that simple beginning grew a friendship staunch and true.

It was a Christmas party for a hundred children which set the pointer for specialised service for the deaf. Two of the little ones were deaf-mutes, terribly out of place among the noisy crowd, and feeling shut out. The two officers set themselves to learn and teach sign language, so that they could communicate. Once the news was passed round — in sign language — that at the Army there were meetings for the deaf, more and more people came.

Not only were evangelical meetings held but also handicraft classes for women. Alice was sometimes needed as interpreter between a woman and the midwife, or between a man and his doctor or lawyer. Sometimes she interpreted the marriage ritual to a deaf couple and occasionally she married them herself in sign language. Outings to the seaside were greatly enjoyed, but it meant a watchful strain for the officers, for deaf-mutes cannot call for help in an emergency.

Depression, arising from a sense of isolation, is often the lot of the deaf, but the language of signs is also a language of love, for one must give oneself with the expressive movements of the hands.

Alice Sigsworth retired in 1956 leaving the Centre in the care of her assistant, Eleanor Gebbie, But only two years later 'Siggy', as her friends called her, had to enter hospital. She was very ill but she brought a glow of radiance and joy to the ward. Cheery greetings, quips, sudden snatches of song when she could manage it, all these enlivened the day for the other patients and the staff. Yet 'Siggy' didn't forget the word of encouragement, the prayer, or the simple 'God bless you' when another woman faced a hard time. As the end approached Alice spoke matter-of-factly with her friend Eleanor, giving her instructions. Her last testament — a verbal one — was typical, 'Pay all the bills and if there's owt left, take the kids to Southend for the day.'

'When she died, it was as though a presence had left the ward,' said the Sister.

Sigsworth Hall is a lasting memorial to Alice, its Penitent Form paid for by gifts brought by those among whom she had worked so long .

CHAPTER TWELVE

'Go and *do* something!'

RETURNING from a night engagement in 1887, General William Booth was shocked to see men lying in the niches of London Bridge, a few rags or old newspapers being their only covering. The night was bitterly cold and damp, with a penetrating mist. His son Bramwell records that when he saw his father next morning he was asked peremptorily, 'Did you know that men slept out all night on the bridges?' Yes, Bramwell had heard about it. 'Then,' burst out the old man, 'you ought to be ashamed of yourself for knowing it and doing nothing about it.' Bramwell mentioned the difficulties of finance, of finding a building, of staffing it and warming it, but the old Founder would have none of those paltry excuses. 'Go and *do* something about it,' he thundered.

And so he did and began the Army's extensive social services in Britain, which include night shelters for the homeless. The same pattern has been repeated in the other countries where the Army is meeting the tragic need among the under-privileged.

*   *   *

Othilie Tonning of Norway wished she had been born a boy. Truth to tell, even her appearance and disposition seemed to suggest that nature had made a mistake. It was only later in her life that the feminine characteristics became more apparent.

The Tonning children, all boys, had not anticipated a little sister in the baby who was to arrive in 1865. One more boy in the adventure-loving group would have been accepted, but a sissy, no! The family lived on a rocky island off the Norwegian coast, where heavy waves pounded and high winds blew all the year round. Father was the lighthouse keeper, so isolation was a part of life which had to be accepted. One ate, slept and worked to the crashing of the waves and the coarse shrieks of the gulls. Handling a boat was one of the first lessons Othilie learnt. Father Tonning had been a ship's captain and it was only in later years that he accepted the more peaceful pursuit of guarding the lighthouse beam. Something, though, of his resourcefulness and dependability came through in all his children.

Othilie's brothers went on from school to college, but towards the end of the last century in Norway that was not possible for women. They were expected to complete their education in the domestic realm. This did not suit Othilie; when she began to earn her own living at seventeen in Stavanger, she started to prepare for matriculation.

'I was by nature free,' she wrote in later years. 'I didn't care about custom, tradition, or what people said. I was proud rather than ashamed to get only the lowest mark for religion, although my father had come from a pastor's family.'

The study of modern literature dispelled any lingering childhood faith. God was dead for Othilie Tonning. With self-assurance she threw over many of the conventions of the time, defiantly getting her hair cut short like a man, and smoking cigars. Yet she confessed later that while she was outwardly protesting and demonstrating, in her heart she was seeking a satisfying philosophy of life. Her goal was nearer than she dreamed.

The Salvation Army had started evangelistic meetings nearby, and drew large crowds, for there was little other entertainment of an evening. Othilie attended once and described it as 'macabre theatre'. But she continued to go, being greatly impressed by the two young women officers who spoke about personal commitment to Christ in such a simple and direct manner. Within her heart Othilie Tonning reasoned that any seeker after truth must at least *test* each new way, so half shamefacedly she began to pray. She was no longer so sure that God was dead.

It was the beginning of the end of her spiritual struggle. Not long afterwards she knelt at the Penitent Form and opened her heart to God. The news soon got round! Local papers ran headlines: OTHILIE TONNING SAVED AT THE SALLY ARMY! The commitment made, the new convert's wholeheartedness in everything she did led her into uniform-wearing, even at work. She started to read Army books to learn more of the movement, and was stirred by Catherine Booth's writings. *Practical Religion, Aggressive Christianity, Female Ministry,* Othilie devoured them all. The Army Mother had a new disciple, one with her own strong principles and energetic character. William Booth's book *In Darkest England and the Way Out* stirred her to the depths. Here was the philosophy of life she had sought. She would give her life to serve the needy for Christ's sake.

In the autumn of 1891 she offered herself for any form of service the Army wished to give her. It was almost like a cold douche to be asked to become the accountant at the Oslo headquarters, but it was only while she was learning more of the movement to which she had surrendered her life. A few months later she received officer-rank and was sent to a corps to do evangelical work. The small group lacked the money even to buy wood for heating the hall stove. Across the wide fjord

Othilie could see smoke from a high sawmill chimney. Indeed, when the wind was in a certain direction she could smell the acrid fumes from the wood-pulp furnaces. Borrowing a boat she rowed with strong easy strokes across the fjord to the sawmill, interviewed the manager and returned triumphantly with a free load of good birch logs, enough to heat the hall for some time to come.

Wherever The Salvation Army begins evangelical work, social or community involvement follows. It was the same in Norway. In 1898 Othilie Tonning was made the Army's social secretary. There were already seventeen institutions of one kind or another. During the thirty-three years of her leadership they increased to seventy!

Seventy years ahead of her time, Othilie Tonning started day nurseries for the children of mothers who had to go out to work. She also started homes for orphans or children in unhappy circumstances, one of these institutions being situated within the Arctic Circle. Helpless old people were catered for in a chain of eventide homes stretching from south Norway up to the farthest north, where for three months of summer the sun never sets and where in the winter all is darkness, cold and storm. For these pioneering efforts she received the King's Medal of Merit in gold in 1910.

Othilie was faced from the start with the question — where was the money to come from for all these projects? The enthusiastic pioneer thought out a plan. She would enlist the help of the big daily papers. She showed journalists some of the pathetic letters which poured into her office, asked them to check up which were genuine, and then to publish an appeal for financial help. For years these newspaper appeals made interesting copy, and with the gifts of money which streamed in many needs could be met.

Salvation Army Christmas kettles on tripods, in which money can be placed for the poor, are a familiar sight in many lands today. The first in Norway was set up on the famous Karl Johan Avenue in Oslo, in front of the university near the royal palace. King Haakon made it his custom, every year, to come on December 1st and drop in a substantial donation.

Othilie Tonning, however, had even more visionary ideas. In her mind she pictured a huge fir-tree gleaming with hundreds of lights, around which young and old alike would gather in the wintry darkness as the first Christmas carols rang out. She appealed to Oslo city to donate the tree and her idea caught the public imagination. So for the past fifty-two Christmases thousands of Oslo folk have gathered for the lighting of a giant tree outside the university on the first Sunday in December. As the carols ring out, accompanied by the Army band, the first coins fall into the collecting-boxes and kettles. It is a tradition which no one would like to see altered, for there the spirit of Othilie Tonning seems to hover, as she was the author of the idea.

Colonel Tonning was not the type to enjoy sitting in a rocking-chair in retirement. Her whole temperament was so vigorous, her mind so active and creative, that she would have pined. It seemed fitting, then, that she should die in harness. In her last moments she appeared conscious of some inward summons, for she was heard repeating, 'Yes, dear Lord. Yes, dear Lord.'

The immense goodwill among the people of Norway which The Salvation Army enjoys today can be largely attributed to the influence and service of Colonel Tonning. The first message of sympathy to be received after her passing came from the royal family. Most organisations and institutions of influence were represented at her funeral, but the greatest tribute of all was the silent presence along the procession route of thousands upon thousands of ordinary people. To them Othilie Tonning had given the best of her large and generous heart.

* * *

In the Army's social services it is customary for officers to staff hostels for their own sex. In France, however, there has been for many years a notable exception.

The pleasure-boats which nightly make the river excursions through Paris are gay with lights and music. The guests relax at restaurant tables over a cool drink or an ice while the voice of the guide announces and describes the chief points of interest.

Near the Austerlitz bridge the steamers turn to complete their trip. In turning, their powerful lights pick out a long white boat nestling low on the water, and the words of the guide are carried clearly over the river, 'There, mesdames et messieurs, you see the barge of l'Armée du Salut, where every night more than a hundred poor men are given free lodging.'

The pleasure-boat completes its turn, the voice of the guide is no longer distinct, but the newly-created waves reach the barge and gently rock its occupants into deeper sleep.

In fact there are beds for one hundred and ten on the barge, but other men lie on benches, tables, and even on the floor. Still more sit side by side on the steep stairs, heads lying heavy on folded arms which in turn rest on their bundles of goodness-knows-what. Oblivion — at least for a few hours — is theirs.

All is peaceful, for the hour is late, for those who have tramped the streets all day long looking for work, perhaps begging for food or searching for scraps in the dustbins.

The tall thinnish figure of a woman passes along the narrow aisle between the rows of double-decker beds. At the stern of the barge she opens the door into her own cabin. The floor-space of the small room is even further reduced by the steep stairway leading to the bridge and a door which is always kept locked on the inside. But Georgette Gogibus, being practical, uses the lower steps of the stairway as a display stand for her few plants. The cabin is simply, even sparsely, furnished with an iron bedstead, a table, three chairs and two wooden cupboards. Lockers are built into the side of the boat, a gas-ring provides her means of private cooking, and in a diminutive annexe to the cabin are a sink and a water-tap for washing.

The barge, though of humble origin, has developed a certain sense of superiority since being acquired by The Salvation Army in 1930. At that time hundreds of men slept on empty sacks in the market-places and on the banks of the Seine, even through the bitter cold of winter, and three nights a week a small group of salvationists made the rounds of those sleeping-haunts at midnight, distributing hot soup and bread to all who would accept it.

Brigadier Georgette Gogibus, in charge of the barge, is not the robust amazon one would imagine was needed for such a situation. Her manner is quiet and reserved, her voice soft. Every night she sleeps in her tiny cabin at the stern, the only woman among about one hundred and fifty men. They include men who are unemployed and in temporary difficulties, would-be poets, destitute youths who have left their homes in search of adventure, and tramps. There may be men just released from prison, and blind or maimed beggars. Their woes are legion but their needs are identical — a meal and a place to sleep for the night.

Brigadier Gogibus has been in charge of the barge since 1950, when it was re-opened after ten years of disuse due to the Second World War. She is now retired but the call of the barge-folk is such that she cannot relinquish the ministry which she regards as a vocation from God. Her warm human sympathies make it easy for those who need help to approach her, and her faith in God links them with a power outside themselves.

And how they respect her! Not one of them, however rough or ill-mannered, would lift a finger against her. She is their good angel.

For a long time she was nearly blind, though it was not apparent to anyone watching her threading her way between the upright pillars of the dormitory or running up the narrow steps from the hold. She knew every inch of the boat, but when asked the time had to raise her wrist-watch to within a couple of inches from her eyes!

How then did she control the entry of the men each night? Aware that a person stood before her, she asked, 'Your name, please?' Then with intense concentration she listened, memorising the name, the tone of voice, and the provincial or foreign accent. An employee at her side recorded the particulars and, before the man descended the narrow gangway steps, she had indelibly registered him in her brain. Next time she would know him. She was already learning Braille to prepare for the long darkness that would envelope her, when two operations on her eyes gave her better sight than she had enjoyed for many years. Once more she can rejoice in seeing the leaves on the nearby trees, the swift flight of the seagulls over the Seine, and the faces of her beloved vagabonds.

Georgette Gogibus was born in 1905 in northern France. She was only eleven years old when her father died, but she remembers him as tall, lean and busy. He was both a medical doctor and a chemist. When not visiting patients he was mixing medicines in the chemist's shop. Georgette always watched with grave interest. Father would measure, weigh, mix, and stir, roll pills, pack up powder, and the tall thin girl watching him would long to be allowed to help but never dared to ask. She graduated after the death of her parents, but the memory of her father swayed the choice of a career. For five years she studied to be a chemist.

She had been brought up as a practising Catholic but, with the break-up of the home, ceased all outward expression of her faith. In her early twenties she was completely indifferent to any claims God might have upon her. But back in the shadows God was working, drawing one marked out for Himself.

In need of lodgings in Paris while she studied, the young student heard of the Army's Palais de la Femme (Women's Palace) with over seven hundred single rooms for working-girls and students. After waiting for a time she obtained a room and settled into the regular rhythm of its life. One day she attended a meeting and heard the story of a salvationist who was caring for lepers. Immediately something stirred in her heart and she whispered to herself, 'That's what I'd like to do.'

Good impulses unless acted upon are still-born and her momentary urge was soon entirely forgotten in the round of studies and simple pleasures. Seven years of spiritual indifference passed. She forgot the touch of God upon her soul.

In the hospital where she was serving as a chemist Georgette met a doctor trained in diagnosing illness by the study of the patient's face and temperament. One day, just for fun, she sat for a 'portrait' by him and was astounded to hear him say that she suffered from a suppressed call to a religious vocation. Laughingly her chums teased her, 'Why not be a Carmelite sister or a Dominican nun?' But the doctor, looking at her attentively, said with conviction, 'No, for her it's The Salvation Army.'

Then, in that very same hospital, when the staff organised a fancy-dress ball, judge the surprise of Mademoiselle Gogibus to find that she was expected to appear as Miss Helyett, a fictitious salvationist in the operetta of that name! Georgette had seen the Army uniform, but it took all her ingenuity to produce a fantastic parody of it for the ball.

After several years' absence from Paris, the young chemist attended an Army meeting, and was conscious again of that tugging of God at her heart. She pondered the pros and cons of a life of service. She had to be frank with herself. It wasn't God she felt called to serve in the first place, but her fellow-men — the poor, destitute, needy. She would find great satisfaction in giving herself to relieve their distress.

At the conclusion of the meeting Georgette asked what were the conditions for serving the poor in The Salvation Army. She was offered a trial period of three months to test herself, which she accepted gladly. She was appointed to assist at the City of Refuge, a massive Army institution in Paris where in the course of a year twenty-five thousand people come for help. The need might be for food, clothing, lodging, legal aid, dental or medical advice — there was no end to the distress in the poorer quarters of the gay French capital. From the reception desk in the entrance hall each client is directed to the service which can best meet his need.

To this City of Refuge came Mlle Georgette, qualified chemist and twenty-eight years old, to learn how to serve the poor and needy. For her the City became the turning-point of her life. For three months she helped to visit hovels of indescribable misery, to comfort and counsel, all the while feeling her heart more drawn towards the destitute. Meanwhile, in the attractive meeting-hall of the City of Refuge, a vital spiritual work is pursued. Georgette was ripe for God and ready to follow His way. Soldiership in the Army quickly led to the Training College in Paris.

The discipline of the Training College is strict, with an almost unending round of studies, lectures, meetings and field practice. Georgette confessed that it was only the call of God as her lighthouse that kept her on course during the storms of difficult adjustment. For one thing, she knew very little about the Bible and certainly nothing of doctrine. She couldn't understand the endless regulations, the insistence upon character and obedience, upon *being* as well as doing. The half-hour of prayer each morning in the silence of her own room seemed an eternity. She wanted to be in action, to serve the poor, love the unloved, visit hovels and wash dirty children. Gradually, though, she learned that she would only have strength for the tasks ahead if she met God in secret prayer each morning and received fresh power.

After her training she was appointed back to the City of Refuge where she spent ten years working with her chosen friends — the poor. No longer did the trained chemist move with dexterity and assurance among hundreds of phials on shelves. She was making up prescriptions of a different category now — prescriptions for broken lives — and the would-be social worker was equipped and inspired by the presence of the Spirit of God.

Then Georgette heard that the barge was to be re-opened as a men's shelter. Immediately she exclaimed, 'Why, that's just what I should like to do! God called me to serve the outcasts and the nobodies.' She got the job.

Watch her at work. On the quayside the men stand patiently in a solid block of misery, waiting for the gate on the gangway to be opened, as a sign that they may pass one by one into the tiny office at the head of the stairs down to the hold. Some men are young. Some are so unkempt as to leave their age a mystery. Now and again a picturesque character appears, like the fellow who presented himself in odd rubber boots, one red, one black, with a frying pan firmly lodged by the handle in one of them. When the gate is unlocked at the set hour the forward surge begins, and with it, the nightly recital of woe.

'Miss, I'm sorry I was drunk last night. It won't happen again.'

'Tonight I have to work but I asked the foreman to let me come and tell you. You'll reserve me a place for tomorrow night, won't you?'

'Here I am again, Madame, turned out once more from my lodgings . . .' The brave smile suddenly fades and the voice ends on a sob.

'My feet are all cut, Miss. I can't walk any more.'

'I've lost everything I possess by gambling — my job and my home. I don't know what to do. I heard about your barge on the radio. Please take me in.'

One man is boisterously drunk and so cannot remain, for the sake of the others. The slightly-built figure of Brigadier Gogibus confronts him and her quiet tones pronounce judgment.

'Monsieur, you must leave the barge.'

Curses, loud and long. Shouts, threats, angry waving of arms.

Again in her mild, level voice Georgette insists, 'Monsieur, you must go!' And he goes.

The gratitude of the men towards Brigadier Gogibus takes many strange and touching forms. She can never refuse their offerings for fear of hurting their feelings. She finds it decidedly embarrassing to receive so many little gifts of sweets, biscuits, cakes, fruit or throat pastilles, fished from pockets of questionable cleanliness by hands that are definitely grimy. Then there are innumerable vases, ornaments and plates picked out of dustbins, and flowers left behind by sellers when the markets close. Each gift is a token of the man's sincere appreciation and must not be despised.

A photographer was asked to take an extensive series of pictures of Salvation Army activity for publicity purposes. He skirted round the united meeting that was in progress, snapping here a placid face framed in a bonnet, there a bandsman absorbed in his music, an old woman listening intently, a child asleep in his mother's arms. Then a pair of hands folded in prayer caught his eye and his camera immortalised. Later it was discovered that they were the hands of Georgette Gogibus: dedicated hands, serving hands, praying hands: her three-fold secret.

*   *   *

The woman officer holding the highest Army rank in 1973 is Commissioner Julia Tickner, who for the last five years has been head of the Women's Social Services in Great Britain and Ireland. The commissioner has specialised in work for delinquent girls and has been headmistress of two approved schools. In her teens at Thornton Heath she was already interested in young people. She gave her scant free time to lead the Army's guide troop there which responded so well that it grew from eight members to forty-five.

Julia Tickner is a woman with a strong sense of serving the whole individual. For her no one is a 'case'. Becoming an officer in 1934, she was appointed to the Social Services, gaining experience in various branches of work. Then followed a period of study at Bristol university where she took the Social Science Testamur.

Even in a Welfare State there are pockets of great need which have to be met by voluntary agencies. The Army emphasis has shifted over the years from rescue to rehabilitation, always with the purpose of returning the person to community life, not just temporarily improved, but with the new dignity and purpose which a spiritual conversion brings. Social Service officers live close to those they try to help. Theirs is no cosy Christianity. They must bear the brunt of hourly scrutiny under the gaze of sharp young eyes. They need a special degree of patience and kindness with firmness, but it reaps rewards.

Commissioner Tickner can relate, from her years at approved schools, what great changes can take place when a girl is given a chance to improve in the right circumstances and under loving care.

It was a phone call from the Home Office in London which first alerted her to the plight of Sally for instance. She was one of a difficult gang that they wanted to break up. In accordance with the Army custom of never saying no if there is a chance to help, Sally was accepted. She arrived at the school wild and untamed in character and appearance. For several months she made life tough for the officers. She would pick a quarrel with one of the other girls and fight without any provocation. Often when she swore very competently, the Commissioner had to say to her, 'Sally, would you try to say it in simple English so that I can understand you?' Then she would grin and make a try. She could not help absconding. She had always done it. And when she went, she went far, often right to the other end of the country. When she was brought back she would be penitent, for a time.

A kind of understanding grew up between Commissioner Tickner and this girl and she began to open up. When asked about her early childhood, she said that her parents were

Scottish and had both been addicted to drink. The only thing she could remember about her father was the buckle end of his belt. He died when she was eight. Two years later her mother died also and she was sent to an aunt in the south of England. The aunt was kind except when she was drunk. Sally determined to get away and manage for herself as soon as she was old enough.

She made her way to London and lived on her wits for eighteen months until the police got wise to the fact that she had 'no fixed abode', and had linked up with other undesirables. It was understandable that Sally had behaviour problems in the approved school.

One day a teacher came to the Principal's office leading a rebellious Sally. She was causing so much trouble that teaching was impossible. Commissioner Tickner continued with her writing, praying silently for guidance and aware of the girl standing on the other side of the room, brows knit and face glowering. After a few moments Sally blurted out, 'Go on, say yer've finished with me, like they've all said before.' That was the cue the Commissioner had been waiting for. Quickly she walked across the room, placed her hands on the girl's shoulders and looked her straight in the eyes, 'Sally, I shall never finish with you. I shall always go on hoping that some day you'll make good.'

Sally knew that the Principal meant what she said. She turned and walked out of the office, but that moment was the beginning of a change in her. Step by step the officers were able to show her that they really cared and that God loved her. The day came when she accepted Christ into her life.

When the time came for her to leave the school, she said, 'I want to go to one of the Army homes for old people so that I can help other folk like you've helped me.' And that is what she did for a period. From time to time she still writes to Commissioner Tickner to say that all is well, even though she has since emigrated to Canada.

Mary's case was different. She still lived in her East London home, but persistent truancy from school over ten years had left her with a limited education. It was thought that a period in an approved school would help to develop and settle her. One day the English teacher asked the girls to put certain phrases into sentences. One of them was 'out and out'. Sadly Mary's answer gave an unconscious clue to her home background. 'My brother knocked him out and out he stayed.'

She too could strike out and swear and spit and scratch. People would cross the road rather than pass her on the pavement, and she brought an unsettling element to the school. A born leader, she would choose a girl as her pal and within a few days the two of them would disappear. No girl had absconded so often. When the police picked her up and brought her back she would be defiant at first, then repentant. At the end of the Sunday evening service she would kneel at the Penitent Form and make a new start, but it never lasted more than a few days. She would choose another mate and abscond again. This went on for months.

One December evening, Mary came forward again to pray and make a fresh beginning after a recent truancy. The officers united in prayer for her and this time the change lasted — for a whole week. The next Sunday evening Mary asked to be allowed to speak in the service. 'You all know that I've been different this week,' she said, 'and I'll tell you why. I used to be mates with Satan but now I've gone mates with God.' She sat down during the silence which followed, then jumped up again, adding, 'That's what you all should do!' One by one as the weeks passed, most of them did. Mary remained a leader, but now she was true to her new faith in God.

She began to discover that life was good after all. In the following January Commissioner Tickner sent her to help the gardener, which was a way of saying that they now trusted her not to abscond. Out in the garden she was asked to sweep up dead leaves. A few minutes afterwards the Commissioner heard running footsteps and her heart missed a beat. It was Mary, but she was running *towards* the office window. In her hand she held a tiny snowdrop that she had found growing under the leaves. 'Look!' she cried excitedly, 'isn't it beautiful? Isn't it wonderful?' Mary had won through her troubles with God's help. She continued to make progress. To hear her pray for herself and for others was always a very moving experience.

Commissioner Julie Tickner's daily problems are no longer the tantrums of teenagers, for under her control she now has two hundred and thirty officers engaged in seventy centres of work. These include homes for children and for the aged; hostels, schools, maternity homes, a training home for mothers and children, residences for students and working girls and the large Mothers' Hospital and Training School in Clapton, London. Problems of insufficient personnel are among her greatest worries. Every day her post brings her new challenges, but she does not always sit at her desk in Mare Street, Hackney. She is out visiting the various centres under her administration, to discuss on the spot how better to serve the people in Christ's name.

CHAPTER THIRTEEN

Among Prostitutes and Drug Addicts

PROSTITUTION is a woman's problem, but it is created and sustained by men, 'imitation love' given in exchange for hard cash. The motives which drive women into prostitution are many, as those who work among them know, and it is an age-old evil that the Army has always tackled.

What of today? The problem has not changed: it has come out into the open. So the Army tactics have changed to try to help the women involved. Here are some of the women officers who serve in the sordid streets of great cities where prostitution flourishes.

Lt.-Colonel Alida Bosshardt of Amsterdam is well known in the red light district there. She has frequented its streets for many years, and thus her face and figure are among the best-known in the area. She claims, too, that she knows all the three thousand prostitutes by sight and most by name, for they regard her as a friend and come to her with their worries and confidences. She can go into any brothel or night-club because she is trusted, and she regards that trust as a most important factor in her work.

As a Utrecht teenager, Alida first attended an Army meeting through the invitation of a friend. The unanticipated result was that she knelt at the Penitent Form and returned home having made a definite decision to love and serve God. After the completion of her studies she helped in local slum work until entering training in Amsterdam in 1934. Then followed appointments in social institutions and children's homes, with frightening experiences during war days.

Her start in the red light district was quite unheralded and unplanned. In 1948 she was called into her leader's office, presented with an Army flag and fifty guilders and told, in William Booth's words, 'Go and *do* something!' Her parish was to be the narrow roads along the canals where prostitutes ply their trade. She is still there.

In the centre of the district is a narrow three-storey sixteenth-century house, squashed between two night clubs. It is Lt.-Colonel Bosshardt's headquarters and social centre. From it she and her fellow social workers sally forth to make contacts with their clientele and to it come the needy of all categories — destitutes, drop-outs, prostitutes, and alcoholics. Alida Bosshardt is mother to them all, but chiefly to prostitutes.

She knows some amazing facts about the gaily-clad girls who sit in the open windows, smiling and waving to passing men. As a qualified social worker, Alida has checked her facts. The most startling is that about fifty per cent of the girls of all ages are married, and the husbands of some of these drive them in to work from their pleasant suburban homes after they have put the children to bed. They are dropped off in the streets around eight p.m. to make their way to the rooms they hire. The business of the night begins and goes on until some time after midnight, and then the husband calls for his wife and takes her back home to sleep it off. Why do these young married women do it? For money, says Alida Bosshardt, to help buy the house, pay for the car, or finance an exotic holiday which lies shimmering in a land of promise just over the horizon. Of course the young wife pays heavily for the room she hires in town, but even then she is left with a good balance in hand. She'll only do it for a few years, just until the family finances are straight. And quite probably she will be able to finish with it then, as she has a husband and a home.

For the single girls, the real prostitutes, it is different. They *live* in the red light district, the one room with its window propped open being their only home. Lt.-Colonel Bosshardt affirms with strong conviction that girls from happy, harmonious backgrounds rarely start as prostitutes. It is those from broken homes and squabbling parents who run away and settle for the best-paying job they can find. And prostitution pays well when you are young and reasonably good looking: twenty pounds a day is considered the average income. High rents, smart clothes, cosmetics, food, still leave a good lump sum in hand, very alluring in these days of materialism.

In 1965 a wide-awake journalist, sitting drinking beer in a bar, caught a marvellous photographic scoop. Alida Bosshardt in her bonnet was a well-known figure as she sold her Army papers and made contacts, but who was this with her? Suddenly he realised the truth and dashed to his car for his camera just in time to get a picture of Colonel Bosshardt and her companion, who was none other than Crown Princess Beatrix of the Netherlands, dressed simply, in the hope of avoiding recognition. Her Royal Highness became interested in what was being done in the red light district when, as a student at Leiden University, she heard Lt.-Colonel Bosshardt's lectures on social work. She had asked if she might accompany the Colonel incognito on one of her evening rounds. If Alida Bosshardt herself had not been so well known, it is probable that the royal escapade would have passed unnoticed.

At Christmas every year the Colonel throws a party for prostitutes, a giant supper at two a.m. when their work for the night is finished. Nothing stronger than cocoa is served, but hundreds of the girls attend, relaxing in the pleasant warmth of the gaily decorated hall and listening quite eagerly to the Christmas message and carols.

Alida Bosshardt is not only a social worker; she also has a definite evangelical aim in all she does. In addition to private counselling there is group therapy. Between fifty and a hundred prostitutes give up their dubious calling each year, many because of age, but the gaps are quickly filled by newcomers. A half-dozen or so of the girls are converted each year and a few even become salvationists.

Sometimes there is a funeral for the Colonel to conduct, occasionally after a murder. There is a close fellowship in the red light district, a strong feeling of belonging and kinship. The girls really and truly share each others' joys and sorrows. Once when Colonel Bosshardt conducted the funeral of a twenty-nine-year-old woman who had been murdered, more than a hundred prostitutes attended the service. At other times she has the joy of marrying one of the girls — a real love story — as happened with one girl who, by her earnings, was keeping one of her favourite clients at university. When he got his degree they married and now live in a quiet country town and attend the local church.

Not only girls seek out Colonel Bosshardt when they meet trouble. Her competent and friendly approach makes it easy for young men to turn to her, too. One was a former divinity student who had fallen under the temptation of the open window and the beckoning smiling girl. At first it was just an adventure; then it became a habit and self-loathing darkened his sky. Colonel Bosshardt tried to show him that by God's power there could be a new life for him, but he had lost his self-respect and his courage. Finally he commited suicide.

The Colonel is a favourite subject for television and radio programmes and is often quoted in books and the press. When her activities were featured in the 'This is Your Life' series, so many gifts of money poured into Leadquarters that another house in the red light district could be purchased, not far from the first, and a second Goodwill Centre established, providing a much-needed meeting-hall, with side-rooms for handicrafts and children's groups.

A friend who stayed a week with Lt.-Colonel Alida Bosshardt recently said it was like living in a circus. Movement, thrills, emotional stress, noise and colour — all were there. As the two returned to the Centre one day, they noticed a girl ahead of them hobbling along on very high heels which seemed to hurt her. Colonel Bosshardt recognised her as a prostitute and calling her by name said, 'Look, you've got farther to go than I have. I'm nearly home. Take my shoes,' and she drew off her shoes and gave them to the girl who received them thankfully. The Colonel made the last few yards in her stockinged feet quite unconcernedly. Her friend prophesied, 'You'll never see those shoes again.' But she was proved wrong. Next day the girl returned the shoes to their owner.

Alida Bosshardt has only one absorbing interest — to remain in the red light district as long as possible and to endeavour to meet all the clamant needs of 'her girls'. For single-minded devotion to her task she was appointed a Knight of the Order of Oranje-Nassau in 1966.

* * *

The problems of prostitution are the same in the New World as in the Old. Possibly there is even greater promiscuity because of the many races and nationalities that mingle in a land such as Brazil. It became a challenge to the young Norwegian Captain

Helene Löndahl. She had not planned to be a missionary, but she felt God's call and at last made a somewhat unwilling response. Arriving in Brazil in 1934 she threw herself with energy into the task of learning Portuguese and sampling conditions of life among the poor. She was appalled by the fate of young girls, inveigled into the white-slave traffic and made pregnant by passing sailors of any and every nationality. Thrown out of their homes because of lack of space, the girls had nowhere to go for their babies to be born and no one to stand by them.

Helene Löndahl had gumption and courage. She tackled the immediate need by finding a temporary home for unmarried mothers. At the same time she vowed to herself to bring about better legislation against prostitution. There was only one way to do that: she must study the subject and qualify. All her spare hours were spent at São Paulo University where she acquired Portuguese so proficiently that she gained a Master of Science degree in that language. Now began her long fight to better the position of the young prostitutes so piteously exploited.

One objective was a home, not only one where the girls could stay until their babies were born, but where they could remain, the children growing up in the same house while the mothers went out to work. For such a building she needed money. Helene Löndahl had her own way of getting donations. Having explained with great enthusiasm her plans to a prospective subscriber, she would listen gravely while he offered her a certain amount. Then she would rise and say, 'I'm sorry. I couldn't take that. It's not enough!' Her ruse on behalf of her protégées usually brought a substantial increase. If not, she returned another day.

It was a proud moment for her when the spacious many-roomed house Rancho do Senhor (the Lord's Ranch) was inaugurated in São Paulo. In the large garden surrounding the house a row of seven tiny cottages has been built. They look a little crazy, leaning puckishly against each other, their quaint roofs making an uneven line. They are the Houses of the Seven Dwarfs for the children to play in, away from the big house. Each little cottage bears the name of a dwarf with his face modelled on the gable. It all adds up to a feeling of being wanted and loved at the Lord's Ranch.

Colonel Löndahl's continued efforts awoke the conscience of the nation, and soon grants were made to the Lord's Ranch both from the authorities and the churches. But it took fifteen years of fight and pressure before her efforts brought fruit in the passing of a law prohibiting prostitution. When the date came for the signing of the new law, Colonel Löndahl had been transferred to South Africa in charge of the Army's Social Services for women, but the Brazilian government specially invited her to be present at the momentous happening to which she had so largely contributed. She was also awarded Brazil's Medal of Honour, and for her social work among prostitutes and unmarried mothers she was honoured by the King of Norway with the St. Olav Medal for Distinguished Service.

Announcing her retirement from her last appointment in Sweden, Colonel Löndahl wrote, 'What a rich life mine has been. I would not call it an easy one, but how interesting! God called me to be a fighter in an Army whose Founder said, "Go and *do* something about it." '

After retiring, the Colonel undertook a tour of inspection of the social institutions of South America on behalf of the United Nations Organisation, before illness preceded her passing away.

*   *   *

Prostitution and its related problems, though evil in themselves, seem to dwindle in the face of drug-addiction, the latest, most frightening abyss opening before unwary feet. The craving for a 'fix' shreds away all barriers of moral rectitude, leading to stealing, lying, even brutal assault on the aged or children, for the sake of paltry cash. At the same time the drug addict rapidly deteriorates physically, becoming unkempt, verminous and undernourished.

The Army has always subscribed to the theory that a fence at the top of the cliff is better than an ambulance at the bottom, but what fence can be raised against the 'pusher' who treats school-children to sweets that will 'give them pleasant dreams'? By the time help is sought or the victim is discovered untold damage had been done.

Brigadier Dorothy Berry of New York faces many problems in her attempt to rescue girls and women from their self-inflicted misery. For the 'junkie' is often a scrounger with a vicious temper, possibly pregnant or with venereal disease. Sometimes the girl will seek help herself, knowing that she has come to the end of her tether and that suicide yawns at her feet. At other times her family or friends will approach the Army on her behalf. Even the decision to meet Brigadier Berry to ask for help is a tremendous effort.

Sitting nervously on the edge of a chair the girl is far from co-operative. In a frightened or arrogant voice — much depends on when the last fix was taken — she will give a few facts, usually well seasoned with fancies. She needs money, a place to stay in, clothes and help to conquer her craving. A trained caseworker gathers the particulars. Sometimes the girl refuses to give her name and is entered merely as a number in the record. Patiently, enough of the past is elicited to find out how best to help her. She must be cut off immediately from former associates and all chance of a drug-peddler finding her. So she may be sent direct to the Army's Narcotic Treatment Centre in New York, where there is accommodation for twenty-five girls. Here medical aid is given, as well as helpful therapy towards rehabilitation, by an understanding and compassionate staff.

Women and girls sentenced to a term in the House of Detention for drug offences are visited by Brigadier Berry, and the frequent chapel services conducted by the salvationists help to strengthen the friendly link. A girl wishing to reform will be helped to find work and lodgings. On leaving the prison she will be met by a salvationist who sees her off to her destination. It is a big responsibility to accept such a girl on parole, for the employer must be told of her record. However, the number of cases in which a girl makes good is sufficiently high to warrant the risk being taken.

There was Antonia Paressa of the dark eyes and olive skin; with the background of an unhappy home in the Bronx slums and a sexual assault by an adult, it was no wonder that she fell for the easy happiness offered at school by marijuana cigarettes. Because of her squalid home and indifferent parents the girl was placed in the care of good, well-meaning foster-parents. Their only faults were that they were too trustful, too sure that a nice home and good food could work the change needed in Antonia's life. She hoodwinked them right from the beginning. When she was supposed to be attending classes she was out with a teenage gang, obtaining money for drugs by all manner of illicit means. When her foster-parents realised what was happening they insisted that she should be removed. Antonia did not intend to be caged again, so she escaped, lived rough, got odd jobs as a waitress now and again but most often making the money she needed for heroin by prostitution.

She came to the Army from the courts, charged with soliciting and heavily on dope. For the first few weeks she was hostile to the friendly attempts to win her confidence. Then came a change. It had something to do with her improved health, for the emaciated, unkempt and dirty girl was now clean and tidy, putting on weight and becoming really attractive. A change came in her attitude, too. She no longer resented Brigadier Berry's interest and care. She became co-operative, and the day came when she was found work and a small place to live. It was a try-out in faith backed by the prayers of the staff but it succeeded.

Some years have passed, and in her files Dorothy Berry treasures letters from Antonia, who continued to keep in touch. One of them reads:

I send you a snapshot of my daughter with my husband and myself. When I think of how it was in those dreadful bygone days and how it is now, I can hardly believe it has really happened. We are so happy together and Teresa is such a darling. We go to church as you told me. Best of all, my husband knows, yet loves me all the same!

Another girl's down-drift began with a pregnancy while she was still at school. The news soon got round the small town and although the baby was adopted at birth, Mollie couldn't stand her parents' reproachful attitude and she ran away. She was soon a drug addict and it was in the State Prison that Brigadier Berry saw her for the first time. It had not been her own crime that got Mollie her sentence. In love with a gangster with whom she lived, she willingly paid the price of carrying his gun. In a hold-up the pay clerk was shot and also the gangster. Paralysed with fear, Mollie remained rooted to the ground with the extra gun on her. For that she got thirty years in prison.

With her lover dead and her parents far away, desiring no

contact with her, Mollie was alone. Regular life and food, even though she was inside prison walls, restored her physically and her mind began to blossom. She discovered treasures in the prison library and spent more and more time there. After ten years she applied for parole but it was refused. This was known to Brigadier Berry who was on the Parole Board and who was interested in the great development in the girl. Later Mollie put in another application for parole and this Brigadier Berry seconded warmly, promising that the Army would help her. It was granted.

The day came when Mollie once more faced the outside world. There had been many changes, but perhaps none of them so radical as the inward change in Mollie herself. The years of seclusion, the intensive reading and study, the friendly interviews with the Brigadier who gave her strong encouragement and support, had brought to birth a new Mollie who relied on God for daily help. Sitting in the cab with the salvationist accompanying her, she made a startling statement, 'I want to do something with my life, something useful. It must be work for lepers.'

It seemed an impossible vision belonging more to the thought-world of the prison library than the hurly-burly of life outside, but Mollie was adamant in her purpose. She had studied the effects of leprosy until she felt she was an expert in the subject. She wanted to help its victims.

The final chapter of this surprising life-drama is remarkably peaceful, like a long rosy sunset after a stormy day. With time and patient effort on Mollie's part, and all the help and encouragement The Salvation Army could give, she has become the executive chairman of a group in Washington D.C. which aids leper victims. And she is happily married.

*   *   *

Major Betty Care of the Deptford Goodwill Centre believes deeply in the caring ministry. She has a basic reason for this attitude. A loaf of bread handed over the garden fence by a salvationist neighbour was the contact which led to her father's conversion as a boy in the old Clapton Congress Hall. Tasting the goodness of the newly-baked loaf was a moment that the hungry twelve-year-old lad never forgot. Betty is now in her turn handing out loaves of bread to those in need, both literally and figuratively. She is not so much a do-gooder as a help-you-to-help-yourself person, which is much better in the long run.

She is a mine of information about ways and means of making handicapped people more mobile and independent, from thick-handled knives and forks easy to grasp, to extending metal tongs which pick up articles from the floor and can even hold a floorcloth for a quick clean round. It certainly gives a great boost to the morale of old or sick people to be able to say, 'I can manage!'

Betty Care says that the most interesting period of her service was the time spent in a pioneer endeavour in connection with the Army's Regent Hall corps, in Oxford Street, London. With its central location, the broad pavement outside this spacious meeting-hall is tramped by many thousands of people each day. She was sure that in that vast stream of humanity there would be some down on their luck or in need of counsel. So the idea was born to establish an advice bureau into which people could walk on the spur of the moment. A notice-board outside the entrance invited anyone who wished to make contact to step inside to the office. There Betty Care awaited them, alert, smiling, eager to help and with years of experience behind her.

Surprisingly enough they came! Old people, young people in

groups, sometimes a woman with children who had walked out on a drunken and violent husband, unable to take more, young men looking for work, some of them so weakened by hunger that they had to be given a meal right away before their problem could be tackled. One worried lad was directed to a job which he held until he recovered sufficient poise to be able to resume the studies he had thrown over in a fit of pique. A few dropped in with an embroidered yarn ready-concocted, expecting an instant hand-out, but Betty was astute. She could sense the difference between real need and false.

A coloured girl came in. She was living with her two illegitimate children in one district of London while the putative father lived in another. The girl had been given notice but had nowhere to go. If they had somewhere to live they would get married. It was certainly no small problem, but after a time rooms were found for them and Goodwill officers helped the girl to move with her children. The wedding took place at the Regent Hall, a small reception being arranged for one or two friends. The Registrar was so interested that he attended the reception too!

To cover an even greater area of need an advertisement about the advice bureau was placed in a newspaper. One woman wrote to say that her husband had been ill for two years and was unable to work and she herself was also unwell. A salvationist visited her and found that she was very handy with the sewing-machine. She was rather dubious when the suggestion was made that she might be able to earn money at home by sewing. However, she agreed to try. A couple of months later this letter was received:

Greetings of great joy. My husband started a new job on Monday last and likes it very much. This week I made £10 by sewing and was able to send something home to mother which I have not been able to do for the last eighteen months. I am sending you £1 for any cause you like and I shall always send as business increases. Thank you for coming to my aid in the hour of distress.

One fellow was in despair because his unemployment allowance left very little for food; he had recently been discharged from hospital after treatment for an over-dose of drugs. He was given a small amount of money by the Army to buy some food and pay his fares, and was advised to see the hire-purchase firm to ask for a reduction in the weekly payments. Two weeks later he returned to say thank you for the helpful advice. The hire purchase firm had been considerate and he had got a job as a night-watchman at a wage of ten pounds a week plus tips. Quite without any prompting he promised to repay the money he was given.

One day an out-of-work music teacher called, very depressed and sorry for herself. 'If only I had a piano to play, I should feel more like myself,' she sighed. There was a simple and quick solution. She was allowed to practise on the piano in the Army hall each morning until she found work, which she did about six weeks later.

Major Berry Care found the advice bureau work very stimulating and interesting but she was to change the pattern of her life again. From her enquiries she had long ago realised that some of the young people had a drug problem, even if they did not openly refer to it. But one girl actually asked for help to overcome drug addiction. Betty took her to see a Dr. Peter Chapple, who afterwards became much involved in this work. He admitted her to hospital for treatment. That small event was the start of the Army's Centre for Drug Addicts.

It was decided to begin the new experiment in the Army hall in Chelsea. Partitions were built, and some painting done to make an attractive milieu where drug addicts could spend their days under supervision with trained help. A salvationist of the Regent Hall corps who was an occupational therapist took charge at Chelsea, while Betty continued with the advice bureau, passing on all cases of drug addiction. Twelve months later, with her programme overfull, Betty transferred to the Drug Centre and left the advice bureau in other hands.

With the help of salvationist volunteers Betty was able to build up a worth-while programme for the rehabilitation of young addicts, a pioneer venture that was watched with great interest, and which gave information to authorities all round the world who were themselves trying to combat the same problem.

The occupational therapy was slanted to meet the needs of the youngsters in accordance with the personnel available. For a time there was interest in drama; then art took its place. The boys were at first greatly taken by the mysteries of tie-dyeing, but then that lost its hold. Clay-modelling, talks by an employment officer, group conversations, everything was used that could stimulate an interest in daily life and activate a desire to accept personal responsibility for the future. Drs. Chapple and Grey saw the addicts daily. The Regent Hall corps financed and supported in every way this worth-while experiment to help the God-rejecting, society-cursing, drop-out youngsters, most of them boys.

Betty Care laughs reminiscently as she recalls the meals they served at midday on a shoe-string budget and the minimum of kitchen equipment. It was generally sausage and mash or egg and chips. For three and a half years the Drug Centre functioned, then as the old Chelsea hall had to be demolished, it was decided to conclude the experiment as far as the Army was concerned. Dr. Chapple then opened his own centre for the cure of drug addiction.

Now at Deptford Goodwill Centre, Betty Care is looking round for needs which cry for a solution. She has on her heart such people as compulsive gamblers, a group in real need although they are rarely mentioned. Their lives are as tragically affected as those of compulsive drinkers, and their homes are denuded of all comfort so that they can raise money for gambling. Their wives and children suffer, and for them too Betty feels she must do something. Another opening is a club for the mothers of mongoloid babies. Just the knowledge that they are not alone in carrying such a burden is a help. Holidays for deprived children are also in prospect.

Major Betty Care is making her plans with vision and energy. Her infectious laughter is heart-warming. She radiates good humour and she expects to succeed, for she walks hand in hand with a loving Heavenly Father who cares for His children.

*   *   *

Brigadier Elizabeth Peacocke of Toronto, Canada, is emphatic that her present appointment as superintendent of The Homestead has brought the greatest fulfilment of her vocation.

The Homestead is Toronto's only rehabilitation centre for women with a drug or alcohol problem, or, at times, for prostitutes. There is accommodation in this gracious house for twenty-four women, but day-patients are also accepted — those who have some home obligation from which they cannot free themselves. Five years of experience on this assignment has taught Brigadier Peacocke that the two basic reasons for the plight of the women are broken homes and loneliness.

The clientele, always referred to as 'our guests', comes from different levels of society. There are university graduates and public-school drop-outs, as well as the hippie types. The ages range from youngsters to over-seventies, although the average would be around the forties. Some are married with children, some divorced, some deserted by their husbands. Most of the clients are referred through the usual channels of courts, doctors, Army officers and clergymen, but some women just knock at the door, asking the familiar question, 'Can you help me?'

Brigadier Elizabeth Peacocke is of Irish origin. Emigration to Canada as a child did not change the laughter-crinkled eyes and sparkling humour of her Irish strain. Warm-hearted and out-going, she knows how to make bewildered, depressed new-comers feel at home, and to instil in them some of her own God-backed optimism for a successful outcome. In this haven for the addicted they are given medical and occupational therapy in an atmosphere of loving, individual care. The guests enjoy classes in millinery, flower-arrangement and needle-point, and have themselves helped to prepare a small chapel where morning and evening prayers are held, at which some of the guests have found Christ as Saviour and Liberator.

Brigadier Peacocke has already thirty years of Army officership to her credit, having been commissioned in 1943. Earlier she served with the Army's mobile evangelical unit on the Prairies. This pioneering in country districts was so successful that several new corps were established. Five years of social service in Bermuda followed and later she entered the specialised field of helping addicts. She says herself that 'our purpose is to make tangible the love of our Lord Jesus Christ', and in that spirit she stretches out welcoming hands to those in desperate need.

A French-Canadian Broadway dancer knocked on the door of

The Homestead one day, blurting out, 'I'm beat! Will you take me in?' Her story was a common one — drug-taking leading to crime, then imprisonment. During the agony of her withdrawal, eased as far as possible by medication, the officers stayed with her. Eventually she was cured and stayed on at The Homestead to spend Christmas. It was the first Christmas in her life when she had bought presents to give to others.

One alcoholic phoned the Brigadier saying that she was at the end of her tether and asking if she could be received. Her husband was in gaol and her three children had been taken from her because of her drinking habits, formed during the days of dark despair when her husband was convicted. She was helped back to normality.

Another woman, a Roman Catholic, stopped an Army officer in the street and asked if she knew somewhere she could go to get help with her drug addiction. She had become estranged from her son because of it; this left her very lonely though not in any financial need. When she was received she was a nervous wreck as a result of continual drug-taking. Treatment and compassionate care wrought a cure and the last good news was that the mother and son had been reunited.

The average 'guests' stay for ten weeks, but even after their treatment is completed they are made to feel welcome to call in the evenings or in free time. This gives them an anchor when they face once again a world they knew as drop-outs.

There is a look of quiet satisfaction and joy in Brigadier Elizabeth Peacocke's face as she recounts these stories of women and girls who have been helped through their private hell. They leave The Homestead restored to the community, able to face life's daily demands, and many of them with the ballast which a firm Christian faith can give. Some of them become salvationists.

The Brigadier has given truly sacrificial and dedicated service on behalf of addicts. She was awarded in January 1973 the Order of Canada by the Governor General in recognition of this.

CHAPTER FOURTEEN

Rebellion Among the Saints

ARE women leaders accepted? In The Salvation Army, with its principle of parity between the sexes, there should be no difficulties on this score, yet they do occur.

There seems to be a reluctance on the part of some men to concede that women are capable of carrying leadership roles, able to make decisions with the courage of inward conviction in the face of opposition. Old prejudices die hard and there is often a yawning gulf between principle and practice.

On the other side it must be said that against the innate sense of superiority in some men, there is in some women an urge to self-effacing service. It has happened that when a woman has been asked to take a post of higher authority she has declined, feeling inwardly incapable of its demands despite her excellent qualifications. Both sexes need to adjust in their thinking: men to be more generous in their acceptance of women colleagues and leaders, and women to acclimatise themselves to leadership roles. It will admittedly be easier for the women when there are a few more of them in higher posts. Part of their reluctance to accept administrative responsibility is the knowledge that in any group they will be the exceptions, standing out rather conspicuously in the male entourage.

It cannot be said that there is bad feeling among women officers. Their dedication to God and to service for others is too complete for that. But there is the feeling that their considerable numbers are not sufficiently well represented in top command, in consultative councils and policy-making boards. The present representation of women officers on such boards can hardly be regarded as satisfactory, although it is noted with pleasure that there has recently been some improvement.

All Salvation Army officers, women and men, receive the same basic training for the life-long discipline of their vocation. At the conclusion of two years at the training-college, the broad stream divides into three tributaries. Some new officers go directly to the mission field. These include doctors, nurses, teachers and others who have offered for service abroad. Another tributary leads to social and goodwill activities. Here again are nurses and teachers, social workers and those who feel called to social engagement. The third division is the largest — to evangelical work at a corps. These new officers must preach, organise, visit the people, marry, bury, dedicate babies (the Army's equivalent of christening), lead youth activities and meet their financial obligations. A heavy and demanding programme! Certainly no forty-hour week.

Wives receive the same training as single women. Engaged couples are not allowed to marry until both have completed their studies. In the *Handbook of Orders and Regulations for Officers* (1965) it is stated: 'An officer's wife is herself an officer. She shares her husband's rank and privileges. She is a partner in his life-work.'

Nevertheless, it happens at times that when the husband is transferred from evangelical to headquarters duties, his wife loses her sense of identity as an officer in her own right. The fulfilment of her vocation which she enjoyed while the couple were in the field, made more difficult but not impossible by the care of the children, is limited to any voluntary service she can give in the local corps. Many wives have passed through a period of painful frustration when their opportunities have thus been considerably reduced. Officer-wives represent a vast potential of insufficiently used qualifications, but it is encouraging to place on record that steps are being taken to rectify the situation.

The fact that the wife holds officer-status makes it possible, when bereavement robs her of her husband's companionship, for her to receive an appointment herself. All honour to those who make this valiant response in spite of heavy sorrow.

Here follow the stories of some women who gave the bulk of their service in pastoral activities, and of the opposition which some of them met.

Kate Lee never forgot the happy rapture of anticipation with which she sped to her first appointment as captain-in-command, and the chilly, stony reception which awaited her. She had never experienced anything like it in her years as a lieutenant. To make matters worse, the officer who was to assist her had fallen ill. It would be a month before she was fit for duty.

No one was at the station to welcome her. Well, she was young and could manage her hand-luggage. No laid tea-table told her she was expected at the quarters, but a pinch of tea lay in the canister and Kate made a refreshing cup. There must have been some misunderstanding, she told herself. At the meeting all would be put right.

She set out for the address of the Army hall. Was it that tiny place, hitched as it were to a cemetery wall? Kate's heart, already low, sank further. Soon, she reassured herself, some of the fifty soldiers she knew were on the roll would appear and all would be well. By the time the meeting should start — the moment she had so joyously looked forward to as her welcome meeting — two lads and a few children had mustered. Something was desperately wrong somewhere, but what was it?

Next morning Kate decided to visit her people without mentioning their absence from the welcome meeting. House after house that she knocked at brought no response. Once she was sure that she heard a movement behind the door, so she knocked again, hard. An upstairs window was thrown open and an angry voice asked what she wanted.

'I'm the new captain and I've come to see you.' Kate tried to make her voice pleasant. It was to no avail. 'I'm too busy to come down. Good day!' The abrupt reply and the tone of voice conveyed the message. Kate had been snubbed, quite definitely snubbed. But why?

Saturday evening found her at the spot listed for the open-air meeting, wondering if she would have to speak, sing, pray and preach alone. Then in the distance she espied the gleam of a brass instrument and a salvationist bandsman came to join her. With a relieved smile she walked to meet him but was again aware of a cold climate and a studied indifference. Other bandsmen arrived and the meeting proceeded, Kate telling herself that perhaps it was the way of the folk in those parts and that they needed time to get to know her.

When Sunday evening came and her well-prepared address had fallen into a flat, cold void, she was near to despair. Resolutely facing one of the leading men, she asked him what was the reason for their ostracism of her.

'Oh, so you don't understand,' he replied. 'It's just that you've got on the wrong clothes.'

Puzzled, Kate looked down at her best uniform. There was nothing wrong with it. 'What do you mean?' she countered.

'We're all disappointed. You've got on the wrong clothes, as I said. We wanted men officers.'

So that was it! It was not herself but her sex that they opposed. Kate made up her mind to win them. It was not easy, for they were a clannish, prejudiced group. She started with a social tea for which she baked the cakes. Half of the fifty soldiers attended. Then a tea for the sisters won the ladies over to her side. Gradually opposition weakened, then changed finally to full approval.

A woman preacher's sermon notes seldom see the light of day. They may even be locked away with a small key, from prying eyes, as were those of Kate Lee during her thirty years of field appointments. No other person saw those notes until after Kate's death when her sister turned the tiny key and revealed hundreds of pages of finely written sermon notes. Every page showed care, method and intensive preparation. The titles were in bold red ink and the wide range of subjects was classified for easy reference. In all there were three locked volumes with over a thousand pages of neat, legible, flowing script. Near the sermon notes lay a small, well-thumbed record book, giving in alphabetical order the dates and places where the talks were given. Beside it was a small leather purse holding the balance of her 'Lord's money', for Kate always tithed her modest allowance and kept a strict account of what was God's.

Kate Lee was no orator; her phrases were not polished and resounding. She developed as a speaker during the years of service, but her strength lay always in the direct approach. She had something to say that surged from her burning passion for God and souls. First and foremost she was a soul-winner, from the beginning and right through her life. She knew how to serve the strong meat of the gospel. Hers were never comforting, easy-going sermons. They were challenging, arousing, convicting. She preached to win a verdict, to get decisions, to bring men and women to instant capitulation to the claims of God.

How did she get the time for such thorough platform preparation for the half-dozen or more meetings at which she must preach each week? She adopted a way of life which made it possible, but which could be described only as rigid self-denial over the twenty-four hours of each day. Whatever personal interests she might earlier have followed were put away, sacrificed to her calling as a Salvation Army officer. Her lieutenants would unite in saying that she never did embroidery or knitting, she kept no pet, did no gardening, never went out for a walk that was not part of her daily mission, and, of course, in the early years of this century there were no distractions from radio or television. Not that Kate Lee would have found these modern media a temptation. Her only relaxation — if one can call it so — was the reading each day of one chapter of a good, inspiring book. She read with notebook and pencil at hand, jotting down any thoughts which could be woven into her talks.

Has a picture been drawn of a woman who was so otherworldly that she was difficult to live with? If so, that is quite wrong. Spartan with herself, Kate was kind and understanding with others, and her different assistants through the years all seemed to worship her. She was not only intensely spiritual, she was also practical by nature and orderly in her accounts, tackling problems systematically, and planning money-raising campaigns and carrying them through. But she always gave the spiritual aims priority.

Any corps that Kate Lee commanded maintained a humming activity. She was herself a worker, a militant, and she expected others to take an active part. With organising genius she drew in some who had been half-hearted onlookers, and her converts were trained into recruits and finally into soldiers. Of course there were difficulties, times when the human element in her soldiers showed more than the spiritual, and matters sometimes came to a head. For such encounters Kate prepared herself on her knees. She came from her room clothed with such calm strength and pleasant persuasiveness that seldom did she fail to cool heated feelings and carry better judgment.

Kate Lee had been serving as a field officer for fifteen years when suddenly she became famous. While gathering material in preparation for his book *Broken Earthenware*,* Harold Begbie had come into contact with her. Her winsome character and the fact that she was the key-person in the conversion of several of the notorious characters he described, so impressed him that he wove, through his stories, the luminous white thread of 'the Angel Adjutant' as she was called. Kate was embarrassed by the strong publicity she received, by the many calls to speak in churches and clubs. It was so foreign to her nature, so painful to her, that she felt it rather as a cross than as a crown. 'It is not easy to bear success,' she remarked.

People have tried to analyse the secret of Kate Lee's success in winning rough and sometimes vicious men and women to a life of Christian standards and loyalty to God. She had a bull-dog determination to win souls. When she got a grip on the life of a man or woman, she never released her hold. Her secret sessions of persistent prayer were backed by repeated sallies into the enemy's territory — a slum home, a street-gutter, a corner seat in a pub, or the lowest type of doss-house. Kate went everywhere, seemingly unafraid and never molested. Her new converts would hear a knock at the door at five-thirty or six a.m. Kate had come to pray with them, to bless them in God's name, before they went off to work. To get around her district she used a bike, pedalling away as hard as she could, even when short of breath through her old chest trouble. Visitation was her technique of success.

As if the people known to her were not enough to occupy her

* Hodder and Stoughton.

time, Kate would study the morning papers to see if any family was in special trouble. She would call and offer what help she could give. One day there was a report of a man awaiting trial in the local prison for a serious crime. She wrote to the governor asking to be allowed to speak to the accused. This was agreed to, but to her regret she could not see him alone, as she had hoped. The circumstances were as complicated as they could be. Kate was ushered into a wire cage with three compartments. The prisoner was in the centre one, with a warder on one side and Kate on the other. Trying to establish some friendly and helpful contact with the man through the bars seemed impossible. Kate spoke, appealing to his better self, telling him of God's love for him. The face before her remained as impassive as a mask. She left the prison feeling that her attempt had been of no avail. One thing she could do. She could pray for him.

At the trial the man received a fifteen-year sentence and shortly afterwards a letter came from him. He thanked Kate for her interest. He said that when he returned to his cell after her visit he had thought over all that she had said. He recognised his wrong-doing and had asked God to forgive him and help him to start afresh. His conversion was genuine for Kate kept in touch with him and when, through good conduct, he obtained an early release, she arranged for him to be received at the Army's Land Colony at Hadleigh, Essex. After a period of adaptation to life outside prison walls, he returned to his friends but continued to correspond with Kate Lee, always addressing her as 'Dear Mother'. Mother-in-Christ she was to him and many like him.

Kate Lee's fight against ill-health grew in intensity. Periods of rest after serious illnesses interrupted her field programme, but she never learned the lesson of trying to spare herself, or taking things more quietly. After one such setback, she made what appeared to be a good convalescence, telling her friends, 'I'm good for ten years yet.' Only ten days later she died in March 1920.

* * *

Brigadier Martha Chippendale was a systematic giver to God. Each Friday evening she put her tenth into what she called 'the Lord's box'. One who expressed wonderment that she could continue to give so freely got the terse reply, 'Eh, I couldn't be mean wi' the Lord.' No! She had given her best during thirty-six years of officership.

To start work as a mill-girl at ten years of age was Martha's lot. Her home was in Yeadon, near Leeds. True, she was only a half-timer. She went to school one day and worked the next, but on the three working days a week she had to start at the mill at five-thirty in the morning and continue until six p.m., for half a crown a week! With two hundred whirling bobbins to watch, joining any ends that broke, there was no chance to relax.

Yet Martha was a happy, mischievous girl. That was probably why the small Army meetings attracted her. One night she knelt at the Penitent Form, repeating the Lord's Prayer, the only one she knew. Even that brief prayer had taken a few moments of time and Martha was late home. Her father met her with a scowling face and asked where she had been. Conquering the impulse to spin some story as an excuse she blurted out that she had been to the Army. The next moment she was reeling under savage blows as her father beat her unmercifully. With swollen and bruised face she crept to bed. Teased next day at the mill because of her half-shut eyes she kept silence, but her workmates soon guessed her secret when she bowed her head to say grace over her bread and cheese.

Another night when Martha returned from the meeting her father felled her with one blow and she lay for a time unconscious on the scullery floor. This time she made up her mind that persecution would not deter her from following Christ. Quite suddenly her father suffered a stroke and passed away.

The way was now clear for Martha to fulfil her cherished desire to become an Army officer. She had been trained in a hard school at home; now more knowledge would be given and some of her rough corners would be rubbed smooth. But nothing was ever to quench her ardent spirit. Quick-witted and resourceful, all her latent possibilities were drawn out by the stresses of field leadership. Twenty-two corps is a long record.

Martha Chippendale had a good singing voice and many of her converts were gained through her songs. One of these was Joe of Nunhead. Passing an open-air meeting, he paused to listen to the music and singing. There was the time when he had loved music, but the taste of alcohol had driven out all other interests. Swaying on his feet, his dirty tattered clothes hanging loosely on his emaciated frame, Joe listened. Then the inner urge began to grind his vitals and he shuffled off to the pub. Seeing him lurch through the doorway, one of his mates noticed how ill and wretched he looked.

'Joe, what's the matter? Are they going to burn you next?' he queried roughly.

'Burn me?' Joe was startled by the question. 'Burn me in hell fire? Hell fire?'

A new and terrifying idea shot through Joe's befuddled mind. With unsteady steps he made his way down the road to the Army hall. There was Captain Martha Chippendale on the platform singing *God's Book of Life*, a well-known song with the refrain.

Is your name written there?

'No,' thundered Joe in anguished tones which rang through the hall. 'No! No!' and as he shouted aloud in agony of soul he staggered forward and fell at the Penitent Form.

Before Joe left the hall that night he was truly converted. There was a definite and lasting change in his character. Later on he became an Army officer and was sent to help naval and military men in Gibraltar. Years of useful service followed before he fell seriously ill. As his end neared he wrote to Martha. It was a short, simple message packed with meaning, 'My name's still written there.'

Not all Martha's songs led to conversions. Once she had to use her singing to get herself out of a precarious situation. She and another girl were selling the *War Cry* in the pubs, and they had gone down a passageway to reach a small bar at the end. Half-drunk men locked the door behind them and tried to kiss the girls, while the bar-tender laughed heartily. Martha was terrified, but she kept outwardly calm. Warding off the unwelcome attentions she countered with, 'Now, gentlemen. None of this. I'm going to sing you a song.' And sing she did, a couple of verses. When they asked for more, she agreed on condition that the door should be unlocked. 'Right you are, sister,' they promised. They kept their word and the girls escaped thankfully from what might have been an unpleasant predicament.

In a small corps in the Midlands Captain Martha found the work hampered by debt and by strong prejudice against the Army. She had met opposition before, but the daily scorn and reviling, accompanied often by spitting in her face, came near to breaking her. She was tempted to think of her home and the many pleas her mother had sent, begging her to return to the family. Matters came to a crisis one Sunday morning. She fell on her knees before God and pleaded for help lest she give way under temptation. God came to her with new strength. When she rose to her feet God's peace shone in her face. All would be well. From that day the spiritual tide began to turn.

Then came an unexpected appointment. She was ordered to leave field service and report for naval and military work. Martha Chippendale felt completely out of her element at first, but was an immediate success with the boys. They liked her jolly good humour, her straight talking — not always sweet words but always with their best interest in mind. During the First World War she kept contact with the service-men in camp, naval bases and on the battle-fields. When on leave 'her boys' sought her out for a chat and a prayer at the Army headquarters. Five thousand letters were sent out to Naval and Military Leaguers each month, many of them from Martha. She was a prodigious writer. She wrote to the lads as though they were her own sons and they loved her for it. In 1918 Brigadier Martha Chippendale was made a Member of the British Empire in recognition of her services.

While visiting her home town during retirement, she went to see the spot where she had knelt as a child to be saved. 'Just there,' she said to a friend, 'I knelt between two drunken men forty years ago and gave my heart to God.' A few days later, just after she had made a characteristically cheery remark, she collapsed and died. On the day of the funeral Yeadon Mills closed down and the townsfolk in their thousands lined the streets in loving remembrance of one who began life as a mill-girl in shawl and clogs but became an amazon for the Kingdom of God.

*   *   *

A Russian waif without a Christian name crammed such adventurous living into her fifty-one years that one is amazed. Her parents fled to America before the baby's birth but died before baby Kowitz was two years old. The only inheritance her father left her was a spinal curvature, caused by his kicking her downstairs in one of his drunken furies. When she was two she was adopted by a couple in poor and unhappy circumstances, but at least they gave her a name. For the future she became Jeanetta Hodgen. She grew into a gawky girl, undernourished, big-boned and stooped.

At twelve Jeanetta left her adoptive parents and hired herself out to a farmer near Denver, Colorado. The hefty, clumsy girl made a good farm-hand and might have spent her life at it, had not some child invited her to Army meetings. Now Jeanetta's bad fortune changed. A salvationist in the Greeley Corps felt her heart warming to the dull-eyed, apathetic girl. She gave her clothes and shoes and invited her home to live for a time.

Under the sunshine of love and care Jeanetta responded with her whole being and a transformation occurred. Helping her new 'mother' in the kitchen, Jeanetta revealed inherent cooking abilities and at sixteen years of age left the farm far behind and was installed as a diet-cook at the local hospital.

Drawn by the thought of dedicating her life to helping other needy girls, as she herself had been helped, Jeanetta trained for Army officership and was appointed to a girls' home in Honolulu where she remained for six years.

After homeland furlough in San Francisco, Jeanetta was sent to a sugar plantation where evangelical and welfare work had been started. Her knowledge of diets helped the Filipino mothers to cut down the ravages of beri-beri, and, later, Jeanetta started a school of cookery for the women of the Honolulu groups under her care.

Her most absorbing project lay further ahead. She was feeling her way towards it, step by step, not realising that the urge within her to visit Damon Tract was a vital link in the chain.

For she never got away from Damon Tract again. The Tract was an area of land given by a rich woman in an attempt to solve Honolulu's problem of the homeless poor. About six hundred families had put up primitive shacks of corrugated iron, planks of wood, sheets of cardboard, sacks ... any available thing. Here many nationalities mingled — Hawaiians, Japanese, Chinese and Puerto-Ricans, with all kinds of in-between mixtures.

Jeanetta Hodgen gave up her town flat and moved into Damon Tract to be nearer 'her people', as she called them. A small meeting-hall was erected on the Tract with a little house for Jeanetta, but the premises had to be moved or enlarged four times to provide space for all those who wanted to attend. The 'Mother of Damon Tract' had her hands full from morning to evening. Youth work, classes for adults and, of course, cooking classes were packed into the weekdays, with meetings on Sundays.

During the long idle weeks of the summer holidays the Tract children were often bored and got into mischief. Jeanetta, searching her mind for an idea, asked for the loan of the empty school building. She planned a daily vacation Bible school, with examinations at the end of classes and a public event for the awarding of diplomas. Three hundred children filled the classrooms for a couple of hours daily. Eight teachers were employed to take them through an interesting curriculum. The authorities and the parents sighed with relief. For ten years the school authorities prepared the buildings for Jeanetta's summer use.

There were new problems when school started. This time it was bored babies. Used to the older children minding them while mother was busy, they were fretful and difficult. With thirty of these toddlers, Major Jeanetta Hodgen started a kindergarten and the idea snowballed to another centre which took in one hundred pre-school children. Nine years later it was reported that two hundred and sixty pre-schoolers of mixed nationalities attended kindergartens, led by the Major and her staff of nine helpers.

Then Pearl Harbor became ominous news. Civilians were evacuated from the Tract and United States airmen took their place. Jeanetta had a new family. She drove through the black-out with hot coffee and doughnuts, visited 'her boys' in hospital, wrote their letters and took messages. She also officiated at their weddings and dedicated their babies. She loved to perform these dedications. It must have been a moving sight to see her tall, stooping form shielding the tiny life for a few moments of prayer.

In 1946 Honolulu's Rotary Club presented Jeanetta Hodgen with a gift inscribed 'For the year's most significant achievement in promoting the ideal of service'. Suddenly in 1951 Jeanetta was called home to God. She was laid to rest in Damon Tract with Hawaiian laments and tears of gratitude.

*   *   *

Henrietta Wingett knew that some of the Boscombe comrades were aghast when they heard that a woman was appointed as their commanding officer. Such a thing had not happened for twenty-five years! And it was just when the corps faced a sustained fund-raising effort to provide renovations to the hall, and additional accommodation.

Major Wingett sensed it when she stepped on to the platform for the welcome meeting, but of course the feelings seething under the surface were nicely covered up for the occasion. Extraordinary success had attended Hetty Wingett's ministry in Bridport, where she had built up a fully organised corps out of nothing in two years. So she had experience. And she had good sense and grit.

A Devon farmer's daughter, Hetty was a lay preacher while still in her teens, and was often out driving in the dog-cart to visit aged or sick folk, taking a gift of some of her prize-winning cheese or butter. Her friendly sympathy, cheery smile and ready laugh made an open road into people's hearts. Then came her contact with The Salvation Army and the country-loving girl made the painful transition to London and the training college. That was a trying period for one who loved open skies, green meadows, and animals to care for. It was the price of her dedication and Hetty paid it.

After enthusiastic service in two corps, Hetty joined the training-college staff and delighted in the opportunity to give guidance and aid to new cadets. She was the ideal training officer, full of fun but not frivolity, dealing straight from the shoulder with slackers, and she became greatly beloved. Though well adapted to London by then, she remained a country woman at heart and would make instant friendly contact with dogs and horses in the street. On the tenth anniversary of her commissioning as an officer she wrote in her diary, 'Gave myself afresh to God. Oh, may I be faithful to all that He has revealed.'

The joy of serving God was a theme often on her lips. She gave herself, her time, her talents, unstintingly. That was her undoing. She burned the candle at both ends and sickness, long-lasting and with depression, followed.

Despite still frail health she made a supreme effort to return to active service and was given — rather dubiously — a small corps which it was hoped might not be too demanding on her resources. She succeeded over all expectations, including her own. It was this comeback which led to the Boscombe appointment.

Accepting the inevitable, the Boscombe comrades soon found that Henrietta Wingett was a live wire, indeed a lively glowing wire which could fire others. She radiated a happy religion. She was interested in people, old and young, but if any group got more attention than another, it was the sick. She *made* time to visit sick comrades. In her the pastor and the administrator were combined, so that by deft organisation she avoided clashes that might otherwise have occurred.

For three years Major Wingett remained at Boscombe — three years which saw the halls enlarged and renovated and the corps built up in strength and unity. The atmosphere at her farewell meeting was a hundred times warmer than at her welcome. She could not resist a sly dig in response to the appreciative comments, 'You see, women *can* do it!' She needed some heart-warming in view of what lay ahead.

She was appointed to Leicester, to be the first woman leader there for forty-two years! There again a somewhat dubious welcome changed to enthusiastic support during her twelve-month stay. Later, youth work and women's groups claimed her. Right to the end of her service Henrietta Wingett remained the same lovable, merry personality.

*   *   *

It has always been a strength to Army officers to believe that behind the official order from their leaders to any new appointment there lies the direct guidance of God. Farewell Orders, as they are termed, can come without warning, disrupting the even tenor of the day, opening unexpected vistas, and shaking the known ground under one's feet. Three weeks is the normal period given for packing, cleaning the house, and making arrangements for one's successor; during this time the wheels of the current appointment have to be kept turning. The uprooting is usually painful.

Lt.-Colonel Myrtle Watson of Australia did not get her appointment as field secretary by post. She was summoned to her leader's office. Her reaction was blank surprise. 'But that's ridiculous!' she expostulated in the emotion of the moment. She was assured that it was a definite assignment, heartily endorsed by those who knew the quality of her work.

At the time the Colonel was a divisional commander, the only woman who had held that position in Australia for a long time. Now she was being elevated above her men colleagues, a number of them older in age and years of service. She wondered how they would accept it, but was relieved and encouraged when by phone and letter came warm-hearted support. The only slightly discordant note came from one who told her she should have been sent abroad years before!

The new position gave Myrtle Watson charge of all officers and soldiers who were engaged in evangelical work throughout six States, a very large 'bishopric'. She now had to lead officers' fellowships and seminars, and speak at the annual congresses, giving guidance on evangelisation. When visiting the 'Inland' she was asked to preach at the Sunday-morning service in the large United Church at Darwin. This was the first time the pulpit had been offered to a woman. The church was filled and close attention was given to her sermon.

When it came to policy-making and decisions the new field secretary made opportunity for open discussions, where ideas for innovations were freely ventilated and examined before being promulgated. This gave her a background of support which was a great strength. The biggest burden was the occasional moral lapses among her flock which had to be dealt with. These she found almost heart-breaking, for while she had to act with decision and justice, her love and pity still stretched out to the wrong-doers. None were simply dismissed. She kept in touch with them, caring for their well-being and trying to win them back to better ways.

Lt.-Colonel Myrtle Watson became an officer from Bentleigh, Victoria, in 1934. She is a typical example of a woman with a great capacity for work. Field and training-college appointments were followed for five years as leader for Women's Social Services. To each phase of service she gave the treasures of her well-informed mind and dedicated heart. Such a well-balanced personality was particularly valuable in her contacts with youth. During the war she accepted some responsibility for service-women.

In the higher administrative positions which she held — from her desk and the public platform which was a necessary corollary to the job — her great gift of inspiring leadership came to fruition. She could bring out the best in those working with her. She created an atmosphere of confidence and faith, and her engaging sense of humour (a most necessary qualification for a woman leader!) eased her round any rough corners.

For four years Lt.-Colonel Watson held the arduous post of field secretary, winning and retaining the respect and affection of her officers. The loving concern for others which had been a characteristic of her life now had to be stretched to reach out to many more, but the spontaneous and prolonged ovation at her retirement meeting in Melbourne in 1972 showed that she had amply fulfilled her mission.

*   *   *

Captain Audrey Peters is a good representative of the large number of young women field officers in Great Britain. She might well have felt down-hearted when appointed to Basildon corps for there was very little Army activity in the new town. About a dozen people attended her meetings. But she is a young woman who can respond to a challenge and by thinking, praying and slogging, she found a solution which has brought success.

In moving about among the people, Audrey Peters was conscious of much loneliness and quiet despair, a social lack not met by the welfare state. In their unhappiness people needed a person to talk to who would listen; someone who would help them bear their burdens; and a place where they could meet others in similar situations. Thus the idea of a community centre grew and the initial plans were made. The project snowballed, adding to itself all kinds of new ventures, until the premises available proved far too restrictive.

Four years later the new Centre was inaugurated. By the sale of two old halls, plus a grant, most of the financial obligations were met with only a few hundred pounds still to raise. But there is a desperate need for added accommodation to house homeless families and lads or girls in temporary need of shelter. Full of faith and vision, Audrey speaks confidently of building this second house during 1973. Meanwhile, as an ever-present reminder of the urgent necessity, she shelters a homeless family in her lounge.

The Army's Community Centre in Basildon provides a day nursery specialising in children with difficult backgrounds. There is a club for handicapped adults and to this the elderly mentally retarded are made welcome. About thirty people attend in this dual group and the mixture of the two categories seems to work admirably. There is a mother-and-baby club and prisoners' wives are invited to join it, so that they are not singled out by themselves. The Probation Service transports the prisoners' wives to and fro and is helpful in every way. One evening a week is reserved for families, so that all ages mingle.

The latest development is a local branch of the National Gingerbread Movement for single-handed parents. To this many men come as well as women. Their partners may be dead or divorced or there may be marital difficulties. Some of the fathers have to manage three, four and even five children. One man came having just lost his wife in a road crash, leaving him to bring up the family as well as hold down his job. Imagine a hundred of these single-handed parents with about sixty children who could not be left at home, and you will have some idea of the lively scene at the Centre on that special evening. Each must feel known, understood and welcomed.

Audrey works long hours every day. Her programme usually runs from eight-fifteen a.m. to nearly midnight. On Sunday she has the usual corps meetings and it has been her joy to see the congregations grow, converts being won and new soldiers enrolled. With a small band of faithful helpers round her she is meeting a real and pressing need in a way that spiralled from her own dedicated heart and life. The bustling all-alive programme of the Community Centre has materialised out of Audrey Peters's vision and is a monument to her resourcefulness and faith in God.

*   *   *

The march past of Army women through the pages of this book is ended, but their steps will resound through the echoing corridors of time. The veterans pass on, but each year a new muster of young women, eager and alert in the freshness of their dedication, joins the cohorts of God's soldiers serving under the Army flag.

Bibliography

Catherine Bramwell-Booth, *Catherine Booth* (Hodder and Stoughton)

Bernard Watson, *A Hundred Years' War* (Hodder and Stoughton)

Joy Webb, *And This is Joy* (Hodder and Stoughton)

Hugh Redwood, *God in the Slums* (Hodder and Stoughton)

Sallie Chesham, *Trouble doesn't happen Next Tuesday* (Word Books)

Majken Johansson, *Från Magdala* (Bonniers)

Albert Orsborn, *The House of my Pilgrimage* (Salvationist Publishing and Supplies)

Minnie L. Carpenter, *Women of the Flag* (S.P. & S.)

Minnie L. Carpenter, *The Angel Adjutant* (S.P. & S.)

Madge Unsworth, *Great was the Company* (S.P. & S.)

Miriam M. Richards, *It began with Andrews* (S.P. & S.)

Gladys M. Taylor, *Translator Extraordinary* (S.P. & S.)

Cyril Barnes, *The Rising Sun* (S.P. & S.)

Cyril Barnes, *The White Castle* (S.P. & S.)

Victory Books (S.P. & S.)
  Flora Larsson,
    Ruth Goes to the Congo
    God's Man on Devil's Island
    Queen of the Barge
  Kenneth Tout,
    Mary of Vendaland
Salvation Army Histories and Periodicals